A PRIMER OF ASTRONOMY

T0382367

SATURN, July 2, 1894

PROF. BARNARD

A PRIMER OF ASTRONOMY

BY

Sir ROBERT BALL, LL.D., F.R.S.

LOWNDEAN PROFESSOR OF ASTRONOMY AND GEOMETRY
IN THE UNIVERSITY OF CAMBRIDGE
AND FORMERLY ROYAL ASTRONOMER OF IRELAND

CAMBRIDGE
AT THE UNIVERSITY PRESS
1911

CAMBRIDGE
UNIVERSITY PRESS

University Printing House, Cambridge CB2 8BS, United Kingdom

Cambridge University Press is part of the University of Cambridge.

It furthers the University's mission by disseminating knowledge in the pursuit of education, learning and research at the highest international levels of excellence.

www.cambridge.org
Information on this title: www.cambridge.org/9781107427433

© Cambridge University Press 1911

First edition 1900
Reprinted 1906
Issued with an additional Chapter and Maps 1911
First published 1911
First paperback edition 2014

A catalogue record for this publication is available from the British Library

ISBN 978-1-107-42743-3 Paperback

Cambridge University Press has no responsibility for the persistence or accuracy of URLs for external or third-party internet websites referred to in this publication, and does not guarantee that any content on such websites is, or will remain, accurate or appropriate.

PREFACE.

F OR the pictures with which this little work is illustrated I have thankfully to acknowledge my obligation as follows. To the Astronomer Royal for a photograph of the Sun. To Professor MICHIE SMITH and Professor SCHAEBERLE for their photographs showing features in a Total Eclipse. To Professor FAUTH for his drawings of Jupiter. To Mr W. E. WILSON, F.R.S., for his photographs of the Dumb-bell Nebula and of the cluster in Hercules. To Professor E. E. BARNARD I owe the drawing of Saturn, the photograph of Swift's Comet 1892, the photograph showing the clusters in Perseus, and the photograph of Holmes' Comet and the great Nebula in Andromeda.

I must also acknowledge the kindness with which the Royal Astronomical Society placed these photographs taken from their beautiful series at my disposal.

ROBERT S. BALL.

CAMBRIDGE,
    November, 1900.

CONTENTS.

PLATES.

MAPS.

available for download from www.cambridge.org/9781107427433

INTRODUCTION.

I⊤ is impossible for us now to know what were the earliest beginnings of astronomical knowledge. Many of the remarkable discoveries, such, for instance, as the recognition of the principal planets, were made in pre-historic times. The very earliest allusion which historians have been able to discover refers to them as objects which were already well known. It is, however, reasonable to suppose that the first of all celestial problems which occupied intelligent man must have been the rising and the setting of the Sun. So long as the Earth was believed to consist of an indefinitely extended plane, it was hard to realise that the Sun which disappeared in the West one evening was indeed the self-same object as that which rose in the East on the following morning. Probably this fact alone led the earliest philosophers to the conclusion that however the apparent evidence of the senses might lead to an opposite conclusion, it was nevertheless certain that the Earth could not be an indefinitely extended plane, but that it must be a detached and isolated body so that the Sun was able to dip down under it, as it were, in the course of its nightly journey. Once this step had been taken arguments were easily forthcoming to shew that the Earth was of globular form. The symmetry of the spherical surface would naturally appeal to the taste of the early geometers, and when they saw that the Sun and the Moon were also spherical, then the doctrine that the Earth is indeed a mighty sphere became an accepted contribution to knowledge.

The earliest observation also associates the changes of the Seasons with certain alterations in the apparent position of the Sun. It was obvious that the Sun remained low down in the heavens during the winter, even at noon. In summer, on the other hand, the Sun ascended high in the heavens. Thus it was clear that the Sun was not a fixed point on the celestial sphere, so that even if the phenomenon of rising and setting was produced by the revolution of the celestial sphere, still some independent movement had to be attributed to the Sun. The acuteness of the early observers led them to distinguish the different stars in the sky. They saw that these stars were arranged in certain definite groups, and they noticed the remarkable fact that the stars belonging to these groups retained their celestial positions as permanently as the Alps or other mountains on the earth remained fixed in their terrestrial places. It was natural to watch how these constellations came into visibility as soon as the twilight of evening had subsided. And then a little attention revealed to the early astronomers the interesting fact that the constellations which came into view at the sunsets in the West were not the same throughout the year. They saw that these constellations changed with the seasons. At last it was noticed that when a year had elapsed, the same constellations returned to their original positions. Take, for instance, one of the most remarkable groups, the constellation of Taurus. At certain seasons the stars of this famous group were found to be situated in the West as soon as the light of the departing Sun had sufficiently faded to allow them to become visible. But after a few weeks these stars ceased to be seen, they had passed nearer and nearer to the West until at last by the time the sunlight had declined the stars in Taurus had passed below the horizon. Not for another year was this constellation to be seen in the same position, but then all the phenomena were precisely repeated. A little further consideration pointed out what the cause of these changes must be. It was no movement of the stars themselves. It was obvious that the changes must be attributed to the movements of the Sun. As the Sun advanced in its course it came near Taurus, and then the stars of that constellation set with the Sun. The same was true of many other constellations and hence it became manifest that the stars were strewn all round the celestial sphere, and that the Sun apparently performed an annual revolution in a track amongst the stars. This track was carefully marked out, and the route which it follows, laid down by the sagacity of these early observers, is the circle which we now call the ecliptic.

So long as the Earth appeared to be a body of vast magnitude with regard to the stars, and at a time when the stars and other celestial bodies were believed to be at no very great distance from the Earth, it seemed natural to suppose that the fundamental phenomena of rising and setting were caused by the rotation of the whole celestial sphere, bearing with it the stars, the sun and the moon, and all the other celestial bodies. But when it began to be realised that the dimensions of the Earth were after all but small in comparison with the distances at which the heavenly bodies were placed, then suspicions arose that possibly this apparent movement of rising and setting must be accounted for in another way. Once it had been shewn by geometers that all the phenomena which were actually observed could be explained either by the rotation of the celestial sphere in one direction, or by the rotation of the Earth itself in the opposite direction, there could no longer be much doubt as to the true explanation. It was obviously more rational to suppose that the Earth turned round once every twenty-four hours than that the stupendous fabric of the celestial sphere with the heavenly bodies upon it could accomplish a rotation in the opposite direction in the same time.

As the Sun performed its annual movements along the ecliptic which runs through the signs of the Zodiac, it was for ages supposed that the great luminary did therefore actually make an annual revolution around the Earth. Here again, however, it was shewn that the apparent movement was really quite different from the real one. Copernicus (1473—1543) pointed out how the phenomena as to the seasonal change of the Sun's altitude in the heavens, and as to the passage of the Sun through the various constellations which mark out the signs of the Zodiac, could all be accounted for in a much simpler manner. He made the bold supposition that the Earth, besides its rotation around its axis, also performs a movement of revolution around the Sun, acccmplishing this revolution in the course of a year.

Thus was our knowledge of the celestial movements advanced to the stage from which modern Astronomy takes its departure.

CHAPTER I.

THE DIURNAL MOTION.

§ 1. Shape and Size of the Earth. We learn in our geography books the well-known fact which demonstrates that the Earth is not the flat surface which a first glance would seem to indicate, but that it is of a more or less spherical form. More precisely we describe the figure of the Earth as produced by the revolution of an ellipse around its shorter axis. According to the best determinations the equatorial semi-diameter of the ellipse is 20926000 feet and the length of the polar semi-diameter is 20855000 feet, and from these figures we easily deduce that the ellipticity, by which we mean the ratio which the difference between the two axes of the ellipse bears to the larger, is 1/295.

§ 2. Atmospheric Refraction. The Earth is surrounded by an atmosphere with a density greatest at the surface of the Earth and steadily diminishing until the upper limit of the atmosphere is reached. The actual height to which the atmosphere extends cannot be stated precisely. It has been found that shooting-stars are sometimes seen at an altitude of more than two hundred miles, and since these bodies are only rendered visible by the resistance which our atmosphere offers to their motion we conclude that the atmosphere must be at least as high as that would indicate. From the astronomer's point of view the atmosphere has always to be reckoned with on account of the effects which it produces in distorting the apparent place of the heavenly bodies by refraction.   Whenever a ray of light passes from one medium to another of different density its direction is deflected in accordance with well understood laws which are explained in any book on Optics.   A ray of light from a star entering our atmosphere at *A* (Fig. 1) is in accordance with these laws bent down through a very small angle towards the centre of the Earth.   We may suppose the atmosphere to be composed of a very large number of successive layers, or strata, lying one below the other and increasing in density towards the Earth's surface.   When the ray passes at *B* from the upper layer to

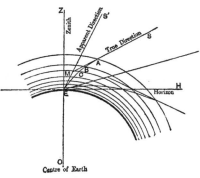

Fig. 1.   Atmospheric Refraction.

the next below it the ray is bent down again towards the centre by a very small amount.   Passing thus from layer to layer it follows a curved path through the atmosphere. The observer is, however, immediately conscious only of the direction of the ray at the very end of its journey, where it enters his eye.   Accordingly, the ray appears to him to come in the direction *S′E* and the angle between this line and the true direction of the star, namely *SMS′*, is called the *refraction*.

A star vertically overhead is unaffected, since the ray of light from it to the eye of the observer is perpendicular to each of the successive strata through which it passes. But at any distance from the zenith, for so the point vertically overhead is termed, down to the horizon, the refraction gradually increases. Thus, for instance, at an apparent zenith distance of 45° the effect of refraction is to make a star appear 58″·2 higher than it ought to appear if the air were absent. Towards the horizon refraction increases, and becomes 34′ when a star is actually at the horizon, but, generally speaking, refraction may be taken as proportional to the tangent of the zenith distance for moderate distances from the zenith.

§ 3. **The Celestial Sphere.** The various celestial bodies are conventionally supposed by the astronomer to be on the surface of a sphere which we call the *celestial sphere.* Of course I need hardly say that the stars are at very varied distances from the Earth, but nevertheless the appearance of the heavens can be represented on a globe of which the observer is supposed to occupy the centre. With regard to the ordinary stars, their distances are so enormous as compared with the dimensions of the Earth, that the size of the latter may be absolutely neglected, and observers in all parts of the Earth may be considered equally as occupying the centre of the celestial sphere.

When dealing with the members of the solar system, whose distances though vast are not so enormous as to justify us in considering the Earth as a mere point at the centre, it is often necessary to take into account the position of the observer on the surface of the Earth.

§ 4. **The Constellations.** The majority of the objects visible in the sky are known as the fixed stars ; there are only five planets which are conspicuously visible to the unaided eye, namely, Mercury, Venus, Mars, Jupiter and Saturn. The fixed stars have been classified according to their degrees of brightness. The brightest stars are those of the first magnitude, such as Sirius, Arcturus,

Vega, and Capella. The next order of magnitude may be illustrated by the stars which form the well-known constellation of the Great Bear. The stars below those again would be the third magnitude, and so down to the very faintest stars which could be seen with the most powerful telescope. Of the first magnitude stars the number is nineteen, of the sixth there are nearly five thousand, while of the ninth there are about a quarter of a million. A star of the first magnitude is about a hundred times as bright as one of the sixth. Stars of the fifth magnitude are faint to the unaided eye, while those of the seventh can but rarely be perceived without a telescope. The numbers of the stars increase enormously as we include the fainter objects. Argelander's famous chart of the northern hemisphere contains 324,188 stars. All stars of the first nine magnitudes were included in this list, and a considerable number also between the ninth and tenth magnitudes. The total number of stars now known must be reckoned by scores of millions.

The prodigious multitude of minute stars is well shewn in the Milky Way, that broad band of light across the heavens. One of the earliest results of the application of the telescope to celestial spaces was to prove that the Milky Way was composed of myriads of stars, generally speaking too minute to be discernible with the unaided eye, but producing by their clustering myriads the luminous effect which is so well known. A photographic plate exposed in a properly mounted camera for a few hours will record the impression of uncounted thousands of stars in almost any part of the Milky Way. In certain places these stars accumulate in such abundance that it seems almost impossible to discriminate, in the coruscating mass, the individual stellar points which contribute to it. Sometimes, on the other hand, we are astonished to see vacant tracts in which few stars are to be found. From the earliest times it was found necessary for convenience in studying the heavens to divide the stellar regions into groups, which are known as constellations. This early method, which has survived to the present day, supposes the surface of the celestial sphere to be covered with imaginary representations of human figures and other objects. By some grotesque associations the bright stars in the sky are made to indicate the forms of the objects. Whatever may be said as to the art or the science of this scheme it, at all events, provides us with the convenience of a special name for each part of the sky, the stars in each region being termed a constellation. We must refer to an atlas of the stars for a description of these constellations, and it will be necessary for the student by the aid of such an atlas to make himself familiar with the positions of the leading groups.

§ 5. **The Diurnal Motion of the Sphere.** The diurnal motion of the stars, in which of course the Sun, the Moon and planets also participate, has now to be considered. Take some particular constellation, and for this purpose the constellation known to astronomers as Ursa Major and to many people in this country as The Plough is very convenient (Fig. 2). It is convenient because whenever the sky is clear this particular group will be found above the horizon. The first observation to be made is to note the position of Ursa Major with reference to the surrounding objects. The observation is to be repeated a few hours later. A very remarkable change will have taken place. It will be seen that the whole constellation has shifted

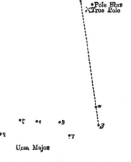

Fig. 2. The Pole and the Pole Star.

bodily. The apparent angular distances of the stars in the constellation from each other have not indeed altered, but the whole constellation has been displaced relatively to the terrestrial objects. A like observation may be made with any other constellation that is visible and in an hour or two the changes in its position will be obvious.

The learner must specially make himself acquainted with that most important star in the northern hemisphere which is known as 'the Pole Star.' It is easily indicated by the two leading stars in the Great Bear which are called 'the Pointers,' because the straight line joining them points very nearly to the Pole. At different hours of the night, or even at different seasons of the year, the Pole Star will always be seen in the northern sky at what is nearly the same elevation above the horizon. The fixity of the Pole Star appears in marked contrast to the never-ending changes in the position of the constellations. We do not indeed say that the Pole Star is absolutely fixed, but the amount of its movement is quite insensible in comparison with the movements of the other constellations.

It would seem indeed as if the celestial sphere containing all the constellations was actually revolving about an axis which passed through the Earth's centre and which also passed, I cannot say through the Pole Star but quite near to it, piercing the celestial sphere in points which are called the North and South Poles. This movement of the constellations, by which each of them appears to complete a circuit of the celestial sphere once a day, is called the diurnal motion. In this motion the relative positions of the stars are unaltered and each star maintains its distance from the pole unchanged except for the small disturbance caused by the atmospheric refraction, as explained above, the amount of which varies as the star changes its position.

§ 6. Circles of the Sphere. It can easily be shewn that if a point on a sphere rotates so as to be always at the

same distance from a fixed point on the sphere its path will
be a circle.   For, if P be the
fixed point and C the centre
of the sphere and if S be any
position of the moving point,
then the arc PS and consequently the angle SCP are
constant. Let fall SN perpendicular to CP. Then in the
triangle SCN, the angle SCN
is constant, the angle SNC is
a right angle, and the side CS
is constant, being the radius

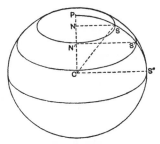

Fig. 3. Great and Small Circles.

of the sphere ; hence the side NS is constant in length.
Also, CN is constant and therefore N is a fixed point.

Inasmuch as SNC is a right angle it follows from the
fifth proposition of the eleventh book of Euclid that all
successive positions of NS lie in the same plane.   Hence
the path of S must be some plane curve, and since NS is
constant in length and N a fixed point, it must be a circle.

Thus we see that every star will appear to describe a
circle, and the planes of all these circles will be parallel to
each other, for the same line (viz. CP, the polar axis) is
perpendicular to them all.   Circles such as those described
by the stars S and S' (Fig. 3) whose planes do not pass
through the centre of the sphere are called *small circles*,
their radii, as NS, $N'S'$, being less than that of the sphere.
Any circle on the sphere whose plane passes through the
centre is called a *great circle*, and it is clear from the
figure that if the angular distance of a star from the pole
be exactly a right angle (or 90°) the plane of its diurnal
circle will pass through the centre and hence its track will
be a *great* circle.   This particular great circle which is everywhere 90° from the pole is a very important one in astronomy.
It is called the *celestial equator* or simply the *equator*.

We may therefore state generally that the apparent diurnal motions of the stars, and here we must include also the Sun, the Moon and the planets, are performed in small circles of the celestial sphere, and all these small circles lie in a system of planes parallel to the celestial equator. It is to be noted that so far as the stars are concerned each one moves round in its circle with uniform velocity and each star also requires the same time for the completion of its circuit, that time being found by observation to be 23 hrs. 56 mins. 4 secs. The times required by the Sun, the Moon and the planets vary.

There are other circles on the celestial sphere which it is necessary for the student to understand. A line hung vertically with a weight at the end determines a direction which pointing upwards indicates the point of the sphere already referred to as the *zenith* and pointing downwards indicates the point on the celestial sphere known as the *nadir*. A plane perpendicular to this line through the observer's eye cuts the celestial sphere in the great circle which we call the *horizon*. If a great circle be drawn through the pole of the

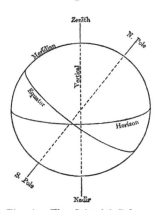

Fig. 4.   The Celestial Sphere.

heavens and the zenith and be continued round, it would pass also through the nadir. This circle is called the *meridian* of the place of observation. Another important circle, as I have already pointed out, is that which is at every point 90° distant from the Pole. This great circle is spoken of as the *equator*.

§ 7. The Sidereal Day. The period of revolution of

each of the stars in this diurnal motion being the same, the result is that the whole sidereal system revolves as if all the bodies were in one piece. The time taken for this revolution is constant. It furnishes therefore a most important natural unit. Its length measured in ordinary solar time is 23 hrs. 56 mins. 4 secs. and this is the period known to astronomers as the sidereal day. Like our ordinary day the sidereal day is divided into 24 (sidereal) hours, each hour into 60 minutes and each minute into 60 seconds. The standard clock in the Observatory is regulated to keep this time, *sidereal time* as it is called. The ordinary time convenient for civil purposes, and which is known as *mean solar time*, has a day nearly four minutes longer than the sidereal day.

§ 8. **The Rotation of the Earth.** It would of course be possible to account for this diurnal rotation of the heavens so far as the mere geometrical phenomena are concerned, by supposing that the whole celestial sphere did actually turn round as it appears to do. We must however always be prepared in the study of astronomy to distinguish between apparent motions and real motions. A little consideration will shew that all the phenomena of the diurnal movement can be accounted for by the supposition that the celestial sphere remains at rest, but that the Earth at the centre is rotating uniformly in the opposite direction, and accomplishing each complete rotation round its axis in the period of 23 hrs. 56 mins. 4 secs. Once the issue has been placed in this way it is impossible to hesitate as to whether the phenomenon should be explained by the rotation of the celestial sphere or by the rotation of the Earth. When it was understood that the various celestial bodies were situated at widely different distances and that some of those distances were excessively great, it soon became plain that it would be hardly short of miraculous if the whole system revolved around the Earth in such a manner that every star, no matter what its distance, should take precisely the same time to complete the circuit. The velocities also with which the various bodies would have to be endowed in order to accomplish such a revolution would be exceedingly great. Take, for instance, the case of the Sun. It would be preposterous to suppose that this body, between one and two million times bigger than the Earth, should whirl round the Earth once each day at a distance of nearly ninety-three million miles, when all the observed phenomena could be equally well accounted for by the much simpler supposition that the Earth is itself in rotation. This then is the first great step in our comprehension of the heavens. It is to learn that this diurnal movement is merely apparent and that what actually takes place is a rotation of the Earth.

§ 9. **Fundamental Observation.** The fundamental observation in the Observatory consists in determining the place of a celestial body, say, for instance, a star. Let it be supposed that we want to determine the position of the star named Vega. To indicate its place on the celestial sphere we must know first of all its distance from the Pole. That is to say, of course, the number of degrees in the distance between the point on the celestial sphere that we call the Pole, and the point which is occupied by the star Vega. This is one of the elements in the determination of the place of the star, but it is of course not sufficient by itself. It merely points out a certain small circle on the sphere (*VA*, Fig. 5), every point of this small circle being at the same distance from the Pole, and the observation tells

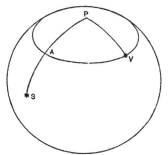

Fig. 5.   Right Ascension and Declination.

us that the star Vega is somewhere or other along the circumference of this small circle. We must determine the position of the star upon the small circle and for this purpose we require to mark some point of reference upon it. Let us take some star as a standard of reference; let us say, for instance, the bright star Sirius, and mark its place on the celestial sphere by the letter S and now draw the great circle PS through the Pole and Sirius. This will cut the small circle along which Vega lies in a certain point that we may call A. We might select this point A as the standard point on the small circle and the arc AV measured from A up to the position V of Vega would give the position of that star. It is, however, not convenient to measure arcs along a small circle, so instead of taking that arc we shall take the angle which the arc subtends at the Pole, that is to say the angle between the two great circles, VP and SP. We can thus completely determine the position of this particular star Vega. We want to know first of all its distance from the Pole, then starting from the Pole we measure the given distance PA on the standard great circle SP. Through this a small circle is to be drawn with the Pole as centre and then the required angle SPV is to be marked off. This will indicate the position of Vega.

It will thus be plain that for the determination of the position of an object on the celestial sphere two quantities are necessary, the distance from the Pole and the angle between the standard great circle and the great circle passing through the object and the Pole. By the standard great circle we mean a great circle passing through the Pole and some standard object. Considering that the whole celestial sphere is in apparent rotation accomplishing a complete turn once in a sidereal day, it is very natural and it is extremely convenient to measure the angle between these two great circles not in the way in which angles are usually measured, by degrees, minutes and seconds, but to measure it as a matter of time, in hours, minutes and seconds.

§ 10. The Meridian Circle. We can now describe the most fundamental observation of an Observatory. We shall suppose that we have at our disposal a clock which has been carefully rated to keep sidereal time. The instrument with which the observation is made is the meridian circle. In former days it required two instruments, the transit instrument and the mural circle, to make a complete observation of this sort. The meridian circle, however, which is used in a modern Observatory for this purpose is, in fact, a combination of the two.

The transit instrument consists of a telescope which rotates on an axis fixed at right angles to its length. The axis is carefully adjusted so as to be strictly horizontal and to point exactly east and west. When placed horizontally this telescope will point of course to the north; when raised to a suitable elevation it will point exactly to the Pole; when turned vertically upwards it points to the zenith. In fact, an eye placed at that telescope as it is turned around its axis will trace out the meridian on the celestial sphere, and to give precision we may suppose that a single fine thread has been stretched across the eye-piece of the telescope perpendicular to its axis, so that as the telescope is moved round, this thread, projected against the sky, will always coincide with the meridian. Such is the transit instrument, and now for the way in which the transit instrument is to be employed. The astronomer waits till Sirius is crossing the meridian. This is the moment when Sirius, rising up from the eastern horizon, reaches the highest point of its daily course before it begins to descend towards the western horizon. The meridian is marked to the observer seated at the telescope by the line across the eye-piece, and he notes by his clock the hour, the minute and the second at which Sirius passes this line, and records the time thus found.

In the best modern observatories an instrument called a *chronograph* is used by which the time of such an observation can be registered to a small fraction of a second by merely pressing an electric key. He then points the telescope to that part of the meridian at which Vega will cross and waits until in the course of its diurnal movement Vega comes across his field of view, and then he repeats the observation, determining once again with the clock the hour, minute and second when Vega makes its transit across the line in the eye-piece. Subtracting the time in the former observation from the time in the latter, he learns the number of hours, minutes and seconds in the angle between the great circle drawn from the Pole down to Sirius and the great circle drawn from the Pole down to Vega. If he wishes to transform the measure of this angle thus expressed in time, into the equivalent expression in degrees, minutes and seconds, then he can easily make the change by simply remembering that since 360° (i.e. the whole circumference) passes the meridian in 24 hours, fifteen degrees of arc are equivalent to one hour of time. But it will not generally be necessary to make this change, since astronomers always prefer to keep these angles expressed in time as they are thus much more convenient for immediate comparison with other observations. Thus one element of the place of Vega has been obtained. We have now to learn its angular distance from the Pole.

To effect this determination the astronomer employs in all modern observatories what is known as the *meridian circle*. This consists of a transit instrument provided with a circle perpendicular to the axis of rotation and concentric with it, the circle being carefully divided into degrees, minutes and seconds, and provision is made by the help of microscopes to enable these divisions on the circle to be read off with extreme precision. We shall suppose that once for all the angular distance of Sirius from the Pole has been obtained, and we shall accordingly employ Sirius to give not merely the first element of the position of Vega but also the second. When the observation of Sirius is being made the astronomer places it centrally in the telescope at the moment it is passing the meridian. To enable this to be done with precision the meridian circle is provided with a second line in its eye-piece at right angles to that already described, so that when the star is in the field of view the observer, by means of a slowly-moving screw, can so carefully adjust the telescope that the star runs along the line when in the act of transit. He will then read off his circle and mark the number of degrees, minutes and seconds corresponding to the point immediately under the index. Next, when Vega is passing the meridian he will take a similar observation, he will place the telescope so that Vega runs exactly along the horizontal wire and he will read the circle and record the degrees, minutes and seconds, indicated by the reading microscope. He will now subtract the reading that he gets for Vega from the reading that he previously found for Sirius, and the difference between the two will give the difference between the distance of Vega from the Pole and the distance of Sirius from the Pole. I have supposed that the observer knows the distance of Sirius from the Pole and hence he is able, by a simple subtraction, to obtain the angular distance of Vega from the Pole. This observation can be repeated with any other star, or it can be repeated with any planet or with the Sun or with the Moon or a comet. In other words, having taken the place of Sirius as a standard it will be possible to determine with all desired precision the place of every other object on the celestial sphere.

§ 11. **The Equinox.** Such is an outline of the process by which the places of the celestial bodies are recorded.

There are a multitude of other details to be attended to. For instance, the refraction of the atmosphere, as I have already explained, always tends to make a star appear higher above the horizon than it actually is. The observations have therefore to be cleared from the effect of refraction in order to exhibit the place of the star as it would have been had there been no such disturbing effects of the atmosphere. Then too I have spoken of Sirius as the standard point from which all the other measurements were made. But any other star might equally have been chosen as a standard, or indeed, any other point in the heavens, provided it was possible to clearly define what that point was. As a matter of fact we do not ultimately use any star but we employ instead a certain point in the heavens, a point called the *equinoctial point* or simply the *equinox*, which is the intersection of the ecliptic and the equator.

§ 12. To determine the position of the Equator. The *ecliptic* is the great circle of the sphere in which the Sun performs its apparent annual movement. To understand clearly how the position of the equinox is determined it will be necessary to refer to the next chapter, where the apparent motion of the Sun is considered. But it will be convenient to point out here how the position of the equator is ascertained.

It is clear that each star in the course of its daily revolution will twice cross the great circle of the meridian. In the case of most stars the lower transit will take place when the star is below the horizon and therefore invisible, but stars situated not very far from the Pole will be visible at both transits. Such stars are

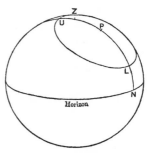

Fig. 6. Circumpolar Star.

called *circumpolar*. Now if the meridian circle be pointed to such a star at its upper transit at *U*, Fig. 6, and again 12 hours later, when it is crossing the meridian below the Pole at *L*, and the two readings of the circle be taken, it is quite obvious that in the upper position the star must be as many degrees above the Pole as it is below the Pole in the lower position. If therefore we add the two readings together and divide by two it is clear that we shall get the reading corresponding to the position of the instrument when it is pointing to the Pole. Here again the influence of atmospheric refraction will slightly modify the result, but its effect can be satisfactorily calculated and allowed for.

In this way we can direct the telescope accurately to the Pole and, since we know that the equator is everywhere 90° from the Pole, we have only to turn the telescope through a right angle to make it point to the equator.

§ 13. **Right Ascension.** The moment when the equinox is passing the meridian is taken as the beginning of the sidereal day and we set our sidereal clock so that at this instant it shall shew 0 hours, 0 minutes, 0 seconds. And if our clock is going correctly then when this equinox comes round to the meridian again the clock should have gone through a complete twenty-four hours and should again exhibit 0 hours, 0 minutes, 0 seconds. The *right ascension* of a star is the time which elapses between the instant at which the equinox crosses the meridian and the time of transit of the star. The clock having been arranged so as to shew 0 hours, 0 minutes, 0 seconds when the first of these events takes place, it is clear that the time indicated by the clock at the time of transit of any star is its right ascension. We are now able to see how convenient the sidereal clock is for the purposes of the astronomer. Each object in the heavens has its own right ascension and we see that its right ascension indicates the sidereal time at which this particular object will be crossing the meridian. Thus, for instance, the *Nautical Almanac* tells us that on May 1st 1899 the right ascension of Vega is 18 hours 33 minutes 33·38 seconds. This means that in an observatory where the clock is going properly the time thus mentioned is the time at which Vega would just be passing behind that line in the transit instrument which indicates the meridian.

§ 14. **Declination.** I have also spoken of the distance of Vega from the Pole as one of the elements to be determined. Now if we draw a line from the Pole through Vega to the Equator that arc from the Pole to the Equator is of course an arc of 90°, and the part of it between Vega and the Equator is what we call the *declination* of Vega. Astronomers have been led to adopt the declination of the star rather than its polar distance as the element to be recorded, and consequently the polar distance to which I have already referred must be subtracted from 90° in every case. This gives us the declination which, with the right ascension as already explained, completely defines the position of the star.

§ 15. **The Altitude of the Pole is equal to the Latitude.** It is easy to shew that the *altitude* of the Pole or its angular distance above the horizon will be different at different places. If, for instance, the observer were standing on the North Pole of the Earth, then it is plain that the North Pole of the heavens would be directly over his head. His latitude would in that case be 90° and the altitude of the Pole is precisely the same, 90°. Or, on the other hand, if the observer were on the Equator

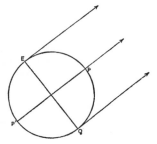

Fig. 7.   Meaning of a point on the Celestial Sphere.

he would find the Pole of the heavens down at the horizon, the altitude of the Pole would be zero, and of course the observer being on the Equator has his latitude zero. As we have seen earlier in this chapter, the distances of the stars are so vast compared with the dimensions of the Earth that we may consider the whole Earth as a single point at the centre of the celestial sphere.

Or, looking at the question from another point of view, the lines drawn from any two points of the Earth—say, two opposite points of the Equator E, Q (Fig. 7)—parallel to the axis of rotation of the Earth, will remain at the same distance apart however far they may be produced. They will therefore pierce the celestial sphere at two points separated by a distance equal to the Earth's diameter. But at the distance of even the nearest of the fixed stars a body the size of the Earth would dwindle to the most insensible dimensions, and two points on the sphere separated by a distance even a thousand times greater than we have supposed could not possibly be distinguished apart. We therefore arrive at the important conclusion that all parallel lines drawn from the surface of the Earth appear to meet the celestial sphere in the same point.

In the adjoining figure the ellipse $EOPO'E''P'$ represents a meridian of the Earth, P and P' are the north and south poles, EE' through the centre, at right angles to PP', is the equator, and O is the position of the observer. Then if the line ZON represents the position in which a plumb-line at O will hang, OZ is the direction of the vertical and OH at right angles to it is a section of the horizon at O. Also it follows from the last paragraph that the line Op, drawn through O parallel to PP', is the apparent direction of the Pole as seen from O. Both of these directions can be experimentally determined by the observer at O. The direction of the vertical is found by the actual use of a plumb-line or some equivalent apparatus for determining the direction of gravity, while the direction of the Pole is ascertained by observing a circumpolar star above and below the Pole as explained on p. 19. The angle *ENO* is actually the geographical latitude of *O*—it is, in fact, by such observations that the latitude is determined— and the angle *HOp*, which is obviously equal to it, is the

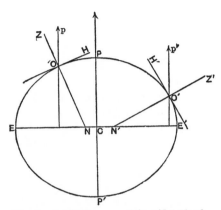

Fig. 8. Latitude on a Spheroidal Earth.

altitude of the Pole. In the figure a second point *O'* has been taken and the corresponding lines are denoted by accented letters. It will at once be seen that the angle *E'N'O'* is, as in the former case, equal to *H'O'p'*, which is of course the altitude of the Pole at *O'*.

CHAPTER II.

THE SUN.

§ 16. Size and Importance of the Sun. Our conceptions of the scale on which the Universe is built will perhaps be best illustrated at the commencement by considering a few facts with regard to the size and the distance of the Sun. The diameter of the great globe is 866,000 miles. To realise fully all that this implies we must consider that it is more than a hundred times as great as the diameter of the Earth. Even this fact will however hardly enable us to form an adequate conception of the vast dimensions of the Sun, unless we further take into account that the volume of a sphere is proportional to the cube of its diameter. It therefore follows that if the Sun's diameter is more than a hundred times that of the Earth, the former body must be more than a million times greater than the Earth in volume. This fact will sufficiently illustrate the proper perspective in which our Earth is to be placed as a body in the Universe. It is clearly of dimensions which must be regarded as excessively small in comparison with those of the great luminary.

The distance between the Earth and the Sun is 400 times greater than the distance of the Moon. It is the fact of the Sun's being so situated that makes it appear to us

no larger than the Moon, which is, as we shall see, one of
the smallest bodies in the System. If we take a globe
one inch in diameter to represent the Earth, then we must
have a globe 9 feet in diameter at a distance of 323 yards
to represent the Sun on the same scale.

§ 17. **Mass and Density.** It may be a little surprising
to note that though the Sun is more than a million times
as big as the Earth, yet it is not so heavy as that proportion
would imply. If the Sun were made of materials which
were of the same nature and in the same condition as those
materials of which our Earth is composed, then, seeing that
the Sun is more than a million times larger than the Earth,
we might reasonably expect that it would be heavier in a
corresponding degree. But this is not the case. The Sun
is only about three hundred thousand times as heavy as our
Earth, and therefore we infer from these figures that, *bulk
for bulk*, the Sun is composed of materials which, in their
present condition, are on the average only about one-third
of the weight of the materials of the Earth's globe.

§ 18. **The Light and Heat of the Sun.** The extraordinary abundance in which light and heat are emitted
from the Sun is one of the most impressive facts in Nature.
The distance of the Sun from our Earth varies slightly at
different times of the year, but, on an average, it has been
found to be ninety-two millions nine hundred thousand
miles. When we reflect how quickly the warmth and the
brightness from any source of light or heat decreases as the
distance of that source increases, we do indeed find room
for astonishment at the quantity and the intensity of the
light and heat from the Sun, which across that ninety-two
million nine hundred thousand miles is able to transmit to
us such warmth and brilliance as we enjoy on a summer's
day.

§ 19. **Figure of the Sun. Sunspots.** The circular
form which the Sun presents to the eye is due to the circum-

stance that the Sun is indeed a globe and, as such, has a circular outline from whatever point of view it may be observed. The first step in the investigation of the structure of the Sun raises the fundamental question as to the physical nature of the materials of which it is composed. Are they solid, liquid, or gaseous? It might be thought that the Sun is a solid globe like the Moon, but raised to a heat so intense that, instead of being dark, and opaque like the Moon, it glows with vivid incandescence. But the telescope shews on a little closer examination that this view must be abandoned. When we study the Moon with the telescope we find on its surface definitely marked features and we always see these features in the same position whenever the observations are made. The objects characteristic of the Moon may therefore be described as permanent. But there is nothing of a permanent nature on the Sun. Frequently the brilliant surface has but little to attract attention upon it; occasionally, however, it will be found marked with dark spots.

> "The very source and fount of day
> Is dashed with wandering isles of night."

The appearance of these "sunspots," for so they are called, is well exhibited in the photograph which is here reproduced, which was taken at the Royal Observatory, Greenwich, on Feb. 13, 1892. Sunspots vary greatly both as to size and form, and exhibit various degrees of permanence. Sometimes they endure but for a few days or weeks; sometimes they last for months. It is thus shewn that the Sun cannot be a solid body. No solid body could exhibit such variable features as are the solar spots. When the photograph is carefully examined it is seen also that the texture of the outer covering of the globe is by no means uniform. The surface of the Sun consists of brilliant white granular parts floating over a darker interior, and the

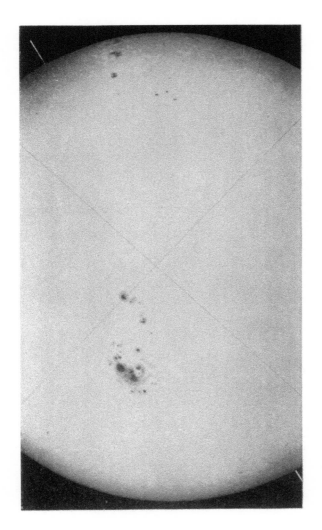

THE SUN

ROYAL OBSERVATORY, GREENWICH, Feb. 13, 1892

To face page 26

glimpses of that darker interior which we occasionally obtain reveal to us the same characteristics as the dark centres of the spots.

§ 20. **Rotation.** Careful study of the spots has disclosed a very interesting circumstance connected with the Sun. The spots as we have said occasionally wax and wane and sometimes they have small movements of their own across the Sun's surface. But it was found by Scheiner, so long ago as 1627, that the various spots all partake of a common movement which could not be accounted for by the supposition of any proper motion in the spots themselves. It is invariably found that they move across the Sun from the East to the West. Those spots which remain visible long enough to enable the observation to be made require about thirteen or fourteen days for the journey across the face of the luminary. Then they require as much more for the journey round that side of the Sun which is turned away from us. And then they appear again at the eastern margin of the Sun. This movement is so universal and so regular that it is obviously independent of the movements of the spots themselves on the Sun. We find a complete explanation of it by supposing that the Sun, in this respect like our Earth, rotates on an axis which is nearly at right angles to the ecliptic in a period of about twenty-five days. We thus notice that the movements of the Sun are much slower than the terrestrial movements, inasmuch as the Sun requires for each revolution a period about 25 times as long as the Earth. It should, however, be pointed out that the period of rotation as indicated by the motion of the spots is not the same for all portions of the solar surface. Spots at the solar equator rotate in about 25 days. Between 20° and 30° of solar latitude the period is 26 days, while spots which break out at 40° from the equator require 27 days to perform a revolution. This remarkable fact affords another proof that the Sun's globe is not composed of solid materials.

When we consider the enormous preponderance in the size of the Sun over the size of the Earth, there is no reason to be surprised at the fact that the Sun's movement of rotation should be so much slower than that of our globe. Even as it is, the equatorial parts of the Sun are actually whirled along three times as fast as the equatorial parts of our Earth.

§ 21. **Periodic Changes in Sunspots.** One of the most enigmatical matters connected with the sunspots is the fact that the number in which they are present appears to undergo a periodical change. A German astronomer, Schwabe, commenced in 1826 a regular study of the sunspots, and after many years of painstaking labour devoted to this subject, he was able to bring under the domain of law the, at first sight, irregular variations in the outbursts of sunspots, and to determine the length of the period in which those variations occurred. From his investigations, as well as from the subsequent labours which have been devoted to this subject, the length of the cycle has been ascertained to be about eleven years and five weeks. That is to say, if we measure from a time when the sunspots are at their greatest both as to number and to individual size, we find that in eleven years and five weeks there is a recurrence generally speaking of the same conditions. In the course of that period, the number of sunspots undergoes remarkable changes. Six or seven years after the time of maximum the sunspots are reduced to a minimum. In some cases they vanish altogether, and then a gradual increase in the number takes place until the ensuing maximum is attained.

§ 22. **Connexion between Sunspots and Terrestrial Magnetism.** A connexion is now believed to exist between the number of sunspots on the surface of the

Sun, and the variations of the magnetic needle on the Earth. This remarkable phenomenon presents itself in various ways and I may mention one in particular. By the magnetic declination we mean the angle between the direction of the North Pole and the direction in which the magnetic needle points if hung in such a way that it is free to move around a vertical axis. At Greenwich, for instance, the needle points about 17° West of North, and the declination is accordingly said to be about 17°. It has been found that the declination is not constant. It varies in different ways, and in particular it has a slow daily oscillation to and fro. Further, the extent to which the needle oscillates in the course of a day on either side of its mean position is found to vary. But the remarkable circumstance is that the extent of the diurnal variation reaches a maximum at the time when the sunspots are greatest.

§ 23. **The Spectroscope.** Many of the most remarkable advances in modern astronomy are connected with the study of the Sun. The information which the telescope has given us with regard to our luminary has been supplemented in a most astonishing manner by the revelations of the spectroscope. We must therefore give here some description of this instrument and its application to the study of celestial bodies. It will be unnecessary for us to enter into special details with regard to the construction of the instrument, or the mode of using it in chemical work, since the spectroscopic method of analysis is discussed in every modern work on Chemistry.

§ 24. **Composition of Sunlight.** A beam of light from the Sun, though it looks so simple, is in reality of a most complex nature. A sunbeam consists not of homogeneous white light, but of an innumerable multitude of rays of light of different hues, the combination of which gives us the colour we call white. These rays are mingled so closely that the complex nature of the sunbeam would never be suspected until special means were employed to separate it into its different elements.

§ 25. **The Prism.** The agent that we use for the decomposition of the beam of light is a prism of glass. It is true that for the higher purposes of modern astronomy the grating, which consists of a plate of glass ruled with an enormous number of fine lines placed very close together— sometimes as many as 20,000 to the inch—and which effects the analysis of the light in a different way, is perhaps the more efficient instrument, yet for our present purposes of description it will be sufficient to refer to the prism. This course will appear all the more justifiable when it is borne in mind that the fundamental discoveries, by which spectrum analysis when applied to the heavens enables us to unravel some of the deeper secrets of nature, have been mainly due to the prism, the grating having come into operation only after the cardinal discoveries had already been made. We may think of a prism as a piece of pure glass, cut into a wedge-shaped form with perfectly flat sides. A ray of light from the Sun or indeed from any luminous source whatever, when it falls on one of the sides of the prism and passes through, undergoes a remarkable transformation on emerging at the opposite side. In the first place that ray of light is bent, or *refracted*, from its original track. The ray is bent always towards the thick part of the prism. If however the action of the prism consisted in merely bending all rays alike it could never have created the method of research which we know as spectrum analysis.

§ 26. **Refraction and Dispersion.** If a beam of sunlight is admitted through a small circular aperture and allowed to fall upon a screen it will appear as a circular spot of light upon the screen. If a prism is interposed in the path (Fig. 9) not only is the spot of light deflected but it is drawn out from the circular form into an elongated patch, coloured red at one end and violet at the other, with the intermediate shades of yellow, green and blue between. This separation of the colours is known as *dispersion*.

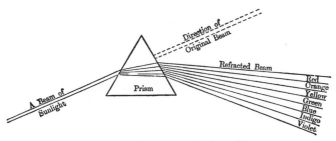

Fig. 9. Refraction and Dispersion.

It may easily be shewn that if we were dealing with homogeneous light we should still find a simple circular spot of light upon the screen. In other words, if we had red light we should find a circular red spot, if green light a circular green spot, and so on. Hence the conclusion is obvious that the coloured patch which is seen when sunlight is passed through a prism is due to the overlapping of these variously coloured circular spots.

§ 27. **Necessity for Narrow Slit.** In order to prevent this overlapping as much as possible and thus to keep the separate rays apart, let us substitute for the circular hole a very narrow slit with its length placed parallel to the refracting edge of the prism, and we shall then have all the essential parts of a spectroscope. It is true that for delicate researches we have to pass the beam through a lens, called a collimator, before it reaches the prism and to receive it in a small viewing telescope instead of allowing it to fall on a screen when it emerges on the other side, but what we see is, as before, a band of colour consisting of variously coloured images of the slit placed very close together, merging into each other and thus forming the beautiful coloured ribbon of light which we call the solar spectrum.

§ 28. **The Ether.** We know that light consists of waves or undulations in the ether, that subtle material which fills all space and permeates all bodies, as easily, to use the famous illustration, as the "wind blows through a grove of trees."

We know too that the colour of a ray depends simply upon the wave-length of the light composing it. Thus the prism in sorting out, as we have seen, all the different colours that go to compose a beam of white light arranges them according to their several wave-lengths.

It will thus be obvious that the prism provides us with a means of examining the structure of any rays of light which are emitted from the Sun. Several precautions of vast importance to the practical astronomer have to be attended to, but they are of a nature so technical that there is no need to set them down in these pages. But when these precautions have been observed, we are provided with the means of examining separately the different rays of light which have been combined together into a single sunbeam.

§ 29. **Use of Photography.** In the study of this subject, as in the study of so many other parts of modern astronomy, the help of photography has been invoked with great success. By the aid of photography we are enabled to obtain in an absolutely reliable manner the positions of many of the rays into which the beam has been decomposed by the action of the prism. But great as may be the use of photography in procuring a record of absolutely unchallenged accuracy, the service it renders to the astronomer involves much more than would be implied by this statement, as will now be explained.

§ 30. **Invisible Rays.** We have said that a beam of sunlight consists of a very large number of rays of distinct character blended together. Those rays include among them rays possessing all the hues of the rainbow. But besides those there are other rays. We have all heard of people who are affected by what is known as "colour blindness." Those who are colour blind have a defect connected with the nerves by which certain particular rays carry the impression from the retina to the brain. Some people are colour blind in some way, and some in another. The introduction of photography has however revealed the astonishing fact that humanity generally is colour blind. That is to say, that there are many rays, and rays of much intensity in the solar spectrum, which are of such a character that no human eye can see them. Thus some people are blind to the blue rays, others to the red rays, while everyone of us is blind to a whole series of rays lying beyond the violet in the spectrum whose existence the photographic plate announces. It is indeed a noteworthy fact that some of the rays to us invisible are not only visible to the photographic eye, but are much brighter photographically than the rays which are capable of affecting our sense of vision. This circumstance has given extraordinary emphasis to the value of photography for astronomical purposes. Not alone will the photograph receive through the spectroscope and record for our instruction many, if not all of the rays which we can see, but it will take rays which we cannot see, and which we have no other means of perceiving, and it will often represent these rays with a distinctness not at all inferior, and indeed in some cases very much superior, to the distinctness with which it sets forth the rays that appeal directly to our sense of vision.

Let us suppose that we desire to obtain a photograph of the spectrum of the Sun. The light is admitted to the

photographic spectroscope as into the visual instrument to
which we have already referred through a very narrow slit,
which is placed parallel to the refracting edge of the prism.
The light enters therefore in the form of a very thin ribbon.
This thin slice of light, if it merely fell upon the plate,
without the interposition of the prism, would simply give a
line of light.   The action of the prism, however, separates
the variously coloured lines of light whose juxtaposition
makes up the spectrum band.

§ 31. **Fraunhofer Lines.**   The first remarkable fact to
be noticed is that the glorious band of colour from the extreme red to the extreme violet is crossed by numerous dark
lines.   These were discovered long before their nature was
understood.   They were noticed by Wollaston about the
year 1802, but they are generally known by the term
"Fraunhofer" lines, as it was the illustrious physicist of
that name who first studied them with care.   He recognised
that these lines were constantly present in sunlight, he saw
that like the stars in the heavens they had their distinct
positions which they permanently preserved, and he saw
that they also differed greatly in their intensity : that they
were in fact characteristic features in the solar spectrum.
Perceiving these facts he attached symbols to represent
these different lines.   The strong line in the extreme red
he called *A*, then came *B* and *C*, *D*, a very famous line,
was in the yellow, and then followed *E*, *F* and *G*, and
lastly *H* in the violet.   Other lines have been since added
beyond *H*, but these are in that part of the spectrum
which is only visible to the photographic plate.

The lines so designated are only, however, the more
conspicuous ones of a very large host.   I have already
likened the lines of the solar spectrum to the stars in the
sky, and we may perhaps carry the analogy a step further.
With every increase in our optical power the stars in
the heavens appear in ever increasing numbers.   In like

manner the number of the lines in the solar spectrum increases enormously with every improvement in the delicacy and power of the apparatus with which the refraction is produced, and with every advance in the delicacy of the photographic plate on which the pictures are received. At first the lines were recognised in dozens or in scores, now they are known to the number of many thousands. It has frequently happened that lines which appeared single in the first instance have by closer examination been shown to be composed of two or more distinct lines so near as to appear coincident. And this process of the discovery of new lines is still going on. By passing the light through a number of prisms in succession the dispersive effect of a single prism is proportionately multiplied and the length of the spectrum and the distance of the lines from each other can thus be increased. Since, however, the light is drawn out thinner and thinner with every increase of dispersion there is a limit to the dispersion which can be usefully employed. The extremely sensitive plates now made by enabling a higher dispersion to be used have greatly increased the number of the lines in the ultra-violet, or invisible, regions, and many of the most important applications of spectroscopic astronomy depend for their success upon the interpretation of the lines set down on the photographic plate in those parts of the spectrum which are entirely beyond the reach of the human eye.

§ 32. **Meaning of the Dark Lines in the Solar Spectrum.** The explanation of the meaning of these dark lines in the solar spectrum constitutes one of the most important and far reaching discoveries which have been made in the nineteenth century. The phenomenon which has to be accounted for is (if we concentrate our attention solely on a single line), that in the composite beam of light reaching us from the Sun, the light of just that special wave-length, which would go to form that part of the spectrum where the line occurs, is wanting. The light of wave-length a little greater is there, the light of wave-length a little less is also there. But that particular wave-length is not represented. How delicate the phenomenon is will be realised if we consider that even though the spectrum were a foot long yet the line in question is so fine that it would hardly be possible with the finest pen to rule a line across that spectrum which would not be too coarse to do justice to it. The point then to explain is the absence in this marked and most emphatic manner of a particular ray of light.

We know that the brilliant parts of the Sun, those parts which send to us the light and the heat so necessary for our welfare, really transmit rays of every description, and consequently the light which they emit if that light could be received by us before it undergoes any subsequent treatment would present what we call a continuous spectrum unmarked by any of these dark lines. The dark lines take their origin in something which happens to the ray of light after it has left the brilliant part of the Sun and before it reaches our instruments. The fact is that the Sun is surrounded with an atmosphere, an atmosphere to us invisible, but extending to a great height above that brilliant region in which the light and heat have their origin. The rays from the Sun, or rather from the brilliant parts of it, have to traverse this atmosphere. This atmosphere is, as I have said, invisible. It is so transparent that it permits the passage of the light without much appreciable alteration in its intensity. But it does not allow the light to pass through without producing some effect upon it. And the effect is of a very remarkable character. It vigorously opposes the motion through it of light of certain particular wave-lengths while allowing a comparatively unobstructed passage to the light of every other description. This is indeed a very remarkable property of a transparent atmosphere, but on its recognition depends many of the most interesting of modern discoveries. The rays thus obstructed are not all connected together, they are in different parts of the spectrum. The consequence is that the spectrum of the Sun is marked with numbers of dark lines, numbers indeed amounting to many thousands, and the more conspicuous of these are what are known as the Fraunhofer lines.

And now for the interpretation of these dark lines. Each line, or rather each group of lines, is due to the presence of some particular element in the solar atmosphere. I may take, as a case for illustration, that most common but important element, iron. The abundance of iron on our Earth seems to be paralleled by its abundance on some of the celestial bodies, the Sun itself included. Owing however to the great heat of the Sun, the iron in that mighty furnace has not only been fused to a liquid form, but it has actually been boiled from the liquid into the gaseous form, so that the iron in the Sun so far at least as this element concerns us at present, is to be regarded as a gas, diffused throughout the solar atmosphere. This iron vapour, could we view it under ordinary circumstances, would be regarded as transparent. It would let the light pass through without appreciable diminution. But when a closer examination is instituted, and when we study the action of the iron vapour on the individual rays of different wave-lengths with the aid of the spectroscope, we then find that the vapour exercises what we may almost describe as quite an arbitrary power of absorption. The majority of rays are allowed to pass unmolested; they pass as freely as ordinary sunlight passes through a pane of glass. But there are certain particular wave-lengths which are in some way or other specially related to the movements of the molecules of iron vapour, and to waves which possess these particular wave-lengths no passage is permitted. To hues of these particular kinds the iron atmosphere is specially opaque; they are not allowed to pass, and there are thousands of such rays. The consequence is that in the solar spectrum among the innumerable lines, there are a number, to be counted in thousands, which are due to the presence of iron in the solar atmosphere.

§ 33. **Coincidence of the Bright Lines of Emission, with the Dark Lines of Absorption Spectra.** A very remarkable circumstance has now to be mentioned. Suppose that we introduce two pieces of pure iron as the poles of an electric light. In the intense heat of the electric arc the iron is not only fused, but it is driven into vapour, and that vapour is brilliantly incandescent. If the light emitted from this electric arc is viewed through a spectroscope, a spectrum is seen which is fundamentally different from the spectrum of a beam of sunlight. In the latter, as we have said, there are the continuous colours of the rainbow ruled over by innumerable fine dark lines. But the spectrum of the iron vapour from the poles of the incandescent iron exhibits a spectrum of a totally different character. In this case we see a number of distinct bright lines, while the continuous, gorgeously coloured band of rainbow hues is quite wanting. By a suitable contrivance the spectrum of the Sun can be conducted into the same instrument as that in which the spectrum from the incandescent iron poles is viewed. In the one case we have the brilliant band with the thin dark lines, in the other case we have no brilliant band, but a large number of thin bright lines. The extraordinary fact is, that when these two spectra are placed in juxtaposition, the position of each bright line in one spectrum is found to tally exactly with the position of certain dark lines in the other. This coincidence is of a most striking nature. It would be remarkable enough if it occurred in the case of one or two lines only, but when we find each one of the multitude of lines in the artificial iron spectrum agreeing to the last degree of precision with the corresponding line in the solar spectrum, it becomes altogether inconceivable that such coincidences could be the result of accident. The explanation of this most astonishing phenomenon seems to have been first suggested by Sir George Stokes, but the general and far reaching law of which it is an instance was discovered and enunciated by Kirchhoff about the year 1860. It is now known that when iron vapour is heated to such a degree of brilliance that it pours forth luminous vibrations, the character of the light that emanates from it is precisely the same as that of the light which iron vapour is capable of arresting. We may indeed illustrate this remarkable property in this way. Iron vapour generally speaking is almost transparent. It levies scarcely any toll on the light which passes through it, except on rays of certain particular wave-lengths. When, on the other hand, this iron vapour is incandescent, as it is in the lower atmosphere of the Sun, the light that it pours forth is composed exclusively of rays of those particular kinds which are absorbed in the former case.

Illustrations connected with music may be given of this principle. The strings in a piano when musical notes are sounded in their vicinity will severally respond to those vibrations which are tuned to harmonise with them. And the particular note that each wire will absorb is precisely that same note which it emits when struck.

§ 34. Relation between absorption and emission. I have selected the case of iron merely as an illustration. What has been said with regard to this metal may, with certain modifications, be stated of any other element. Each element present in the Sun's vapour absorbs light of precisely those refrangibilities which that element would emit when heated. Here then we have the key to the interpretation of these wonderful dark lines in the solar spectrum. The astronomer who endeavours to account for these lines produces artificially, by the help of the electric arc, the spectra of the different metals and other elements. The lines in these spectra are compared with the lines in the solar spectrum. When a case of coincidence is sufficiently made out, a coincidence based not merely on an agreement between a few of the lines, but on the substantial agreement of the whole system, then we have a demonstration of the existence of the corresponding element as one of the solar constituents. The cogency of this reasoning is very impressive to anyone who has had an opportunity of witnessing the extreme delicacy with which the lines artificially produced will coincide with the corresponding dark lines in the solar spectrum.

§ 35. **The "D" Line of Sodium.** The best known instance of this coincidence relates to the famous line "D," as Fraunhofer designated it, in the solar spectrum. This line is in the orange part of the band of light, and is composed of a pair of lines very close together. The juxtaposition of these very close lines is in itself a remarkable feature. Indeed an instrument of some power is required to shew that the two lines are separate. When the comparison is made between the solar spectrum and these two lines which are due to the element sodium, and can be produced by simply placing a little salt in the flame of a spirit-lamp held in front of the slit, or by some equivalent method, the striking coincidence between the two bright lines of the element and the two dark lines in the solar spectrum is at once observed. It is easy to demonstrate that the chances are millions to one in favour of such a coincidence being due to a physical cause, and not being merely accidental. The lines seen in the spectrum of sunlight thus afford the

TOTAL SOLAR ECLIPSE, 1893
(*Shewing Prominences*)
SCHAEBERLE

To face page 40

clearest evidence of the existence of the corresponding elements in the Sun's atmosphere.

§ 36. Chemical Elements in the Sun. This method is employed not only in the study of the Sun but it has been also utilised for investigating the physical constitution of the stars, the comets, and the nebulæ. In fact, it is not too much to say that the whole of modern astronomy has been largely influenced by this new method of investigation. Among the elements known on the Earth which have been proved by this method to be present in the Sun, we may mention calcium, iron, hydrogen, sodium, carbon, nickel, magnesium, cobalt, aluminium, chromium, strontium, manganese, copper, zinc, cadmium, silver, tin, lead, potassium.

§ 37. Appearances during a Total Eclipse of the Sun. We are also largely indebted to the spectroscope for information about some features of the Sun which are too faint to be seen in the conditions of ordinary daylight, and which, without its aid, are visible only when the excessively brilliant part of the Sun is obscured during a total eclipse. A total eclipse occurs on those rare occasions when the body of the Moon is placed directly between the observer and the Sun. It happens by a curious coincidence that the apparent diameter of the Moon so closely approximates to the apparent diameter of the Sun that when the Moon is centrally placed it only just stops out the brilliant body of the Sun, but happily leaves for our inspection the marginal fringe round the great luminary, in which those delicate objects are contained which are ordinarily withheld from our inspection.

§ 38. Prominences. The solar features with which we are at present concerned are the *prominences* and the *corona*. The prominences are usually flame-like projections of a ruddy colour, which often extend for many thousands of miles above the surface of the Sun. They can never be witnessed by the unaided eye, nor even with the help of a telescope, except when an eclipse takes place. It was however discovered simultaneously and independently by Professor Janssen and Sir Norman Lockyer that with the help of the spectroscope the prominences could be observed at any time even without an eclipse. This interesting advance in astronomical art is due to the circumstance that these prominences being mainly composed of incandescent gas, emit a light which, unlike the general light of the Sun, does not contain all degrees of refrangibility, but merely consists of two or three refrangibilities. The consequence is that by the help of the spectroscope the sunlight surrounding these objects can be diffused along the whole length of the spectrum, and thus be considerably weakened so that the light of the prominence concentrated in two or three lines is no longer overwhelmed as it is under ordinary circumstances by the brilliance of ordinary sunlight, and consequently makes itself visible.

§ 39. Corona. The other feature in the solar surroundings which is witnessed during an eclipse is the Corona. This delicate pearl-like light has never yet been seen by any artifice except on the occasion of an eclipse. It is found that the Corona presents some bright lines due to the presence of incandescent gases, one of which is attributed to some element, " coronium," of which indeed but little is known. It is also evident from the photograph of its spectrum that the Corona contains a good deal of material in suspension of the nature of dust or fog, for otherwise we could not account for the fact that it has a faint continuous spectrum, as of reflected sunlight.

§ 40. Depth of the Photosphere. The light of the great orb of day emanates almost exclusively from one single layer of surpassing brightness called the *photosphere*. The great bulk of the Sun which lies within that brilliant mantle is comparatively obscure, and seems to play but an

TOTAL SOLAR ECLIPSE, 1898
(*Shewing Corona*)
MICHIE SMITH

To face page 42

unimportant part, so far as the immediate dispensing of light and heat is concerned. In order to give an idea of the thickness of this photosphere in comparison with the Sun's diameter we might liken his brilliant exterior to the rind of an orange, while the gloomy interior regions would correspond to the edible portion of the fruit. Generally speaking, the rind of the orange is rather too coarse for the purpose of this illustration; it might be nearer the truth to affirm that the luminous part of the Sun may be compared in thickness with the delicate filmy skin of the peach. There can be no doubt that if this glorious mantle were unhappily stripped from the Sun the great luminary would forthwith disappear and cease to possess the power of shedding abroad light and heat. The spots which so frequently seem to fleck the dazzling surface are probably mere rents in the brilliant mantle through which we are permitted to obtain glimpses of the non-luminous interior. It should, however, be said that a full and satisfactory explanation of all the phenomena attending these curious and interesting objects has not yet been attained.

§ 41. **Materials composing the Photosphere.** As the ability of the Sun to warm and light this Earth arises from the peculiar properties of the thin glowing shell which surrounds it, a question of the greatest interest arises as to what particular material it is which is found in this layer of the solar substance. The result is extremely interesting and instructive. It has been shewn by Dr. Johnstone Stoney that in all probability the material which confers on the Sun its beneficent power is one which is found in great abundance on the Earth, where it fulfils purposes of the very highest importance.

§ 42. **Importance of Carbon.** There is no known metal and perhaps no substance whatever which has so high a temperature of fusion as has the element carbon. A

filament of carbon and a filament of that element only
will remain unfused and unbroken when heated by the
electric current into the dazzling brightness necessary for
the effective illumination of an incandescent lamp. Modern
research has now suggested that just as the electrician has
to employ carbon as the immediate agent in producing the
brightest artificial lights down here, so the Sun in heaven
uses precisely the same element as the immediate agent in
the production of its transcendent light and heat. Owing
to the extraordinary fervour which prevails in the interior
parts of the Sun all substances there present must in all
probability be not only melted, but even transformed into
vapour. In the presence of the intense heat of the inner
parts of the great luminary even carbon itself does not
continue solid or liquid. It would seem that it must there
assume the vaporous form just as copper and iron and
other substances which yield more readily to the fierce heat
of their surroundings.

The buoyancy of carbon vapour is one of its characteristics. Its vapours consequently ascend in the solar
atmosphere to a higher level than do the vapours of the
other elements. We can understand what happens to the
carbon vapours in these elevated regions by the analogous
case of the clouds in our own atmosphere. It is true no
doubt that our terrestrial clouds are composed of material
totally different from that which constitutes the solar
cloud. It is of course beads of liquid water associated in
countless myriads which form the clouds we know so well.
As the buoyant carbon vapours soar through the Sun's
atmosphere, they attain an elevation where the fearful
intensity of solar heat has so far abated, that although
nearly all other elements still remain in the gaseous form
there, yet the exceptionally refractory carbon begins to
return to the liquid or the solid state. Under the influence
of what may be comparatively called a chill, the carbon

vapour collects into a myriad host of little beads of liquid, or it may be, solid. Each of these infinitesimal beads of carbon has a temperature and a radiance vastly exceeding that with which the filament glows in the incandescent electric lamp. It is these beads, associated in clustering myriads, that constitute the glorious solar photospheric clouds. The entire surface of our luminary, except for the occasional interruption of spots, is coated over with these incandescent clouds, of which every particle is intensely luminous. We need thus no longer wonder at that dazzling brightness which even across the awful gulf of nearly ninety-three millions of miles produces for us the indescribable glory of daylight.

§ 43. **The Quantity of Heat emitted by the Sun.** The heat which the Sun radiates is shot forth into space in every direction with a prodigality which seems well-nigh inexhaustible. The share of Sun heat that this Earth is able to capture and employ forms only an infinitesimal fraction of what the Sun actually pours forth. The heat and light daily lavished by that orb of incomparable splendour would suffice to warm and illuminate, quite as efficiently as the Earth is warmed and lighted, more than two thousand million globes, each as large as the Earth.

Professor Langley, who has done so much to extend our knowledge of the great orb of heaven, has suggested the following illustration of the quantity of fuel which would be required to maintain the Sun's supply of heat, if indeed it were by excessive additions of fuel that the Sun's heat had to be sustained. Suppose that all the coal-fields which underlie England and Scotland, America, Australia, China, and wherever else coal has been found to exist, were compelled to yield forth every combustible particle they contained ; suppose that this enormous quantity of fuel, adequate to supply the wants of this Earth for centuries, were to be ignited, vast indeed would be the quantity of heat that it would produce. And yet it is perfectly true that a conflagration which destroyed every particle of coal contained in this Earth would not generate so much heat as the Sun lavishes abroad in the tenth part of every single second.

CHAPTER III.

§ 44. Apparent Annual Motion of the Sun. The Sun shares of course in that diurnal motion of the heavens by which indeed every celestial body appears to perform a complete rotation in a period of one sidereal day. But in addition to this diurnal movement, common to all the celestial bodies, the Sun has, or rather it should be said, appears to have, a certain other movement. While the stars remain constantly fixed in the same position relatively to each other, the place of the Sun on the celestial sphere relatively to the stars is in a state of incessant change. No doubt it is not possible under ordinary circumstances, at least without the help of the telescope, to see stars in broad daylight in the vicinity of the Sun. But by observing the fact that different constellations are visible at different times of the year, and that in the course of a year these changes run through a complete cycle, it may be seen that the Sun in that period performs a complete revolution of the celestial sphere with reference to the stars.

§ 45. The Ecliptic. If we could imagine the stars to be visible around the Sun we could mark out the track which the Sun pursues amongst them. By means of the meridian circle we can without difficulty determine the position of the Sun with regard to the stars, and in this way the actual path of the Sun, or rather of the Sun's centre, on the sphere is found to be a great circle to which the name *Ecliptic* has been given since it is only when the Moon is in or very near this circle that it is possible for eclipses to take place.

§ 46. The Zodiac. A belt of the heavens extending for 8° on each side of the ecliptic is called the Zodiac. Within this belt all the movements of the Moon and of those planets which were known to the ancients are contained. This belt is divided into twelve equal portions, each 30° long, which are called the *Signs of the Zodiac.* The names and symbols by which the signs are denoted are as follows :—

♈	Aries	♌	Leo	♐	Sagittarius
♉	Taurus	♍	Virgo	♑	Capricornus
♊	Gemini	♎	Libra	♒	Aquarius
♋	Cancer	♏	Scorpio	♓	Pisces.

The first of these, Aries, extends from the equinox for 30° along the ecliptic, the second, Taurus, from 30° to 60°, along the same circle, and so on.

In the dawn of astronomy when the zodiac was first mapped out the constellations which bear these names coincided with the several signs, hence no confusion arose from applying the names indifferently to the signs and to the constellations. A slow change in the position of the equinox, known as *precession,* is, however, constantly carrying the equinox backwards through the Zodiac so that now after more than 2000 years it has shifted its position by nearly a whole sign. The consequence is that the sign Aries lies almost wholly in the constellation Pisces, the sign Taurus in the constellation Aries and similarly for the others.

§ 47. The Obliquity of the Ecliptic. We have already explained the meaning of the celestial circle which we call the equator, and the ecliptic intersects the equator in the two opposite points which are known as the equinoxes. The obliquity of the ecliptic, as it is called, is the angle between this great circle and the equator. This angle varies somewhat in magnitude but its movements are confined within narrow limits and its value at present may be taken to be 23° 27′ 8″.

§ 48. The Vernal Equinox or 'First Point of Aries.' At the date of the vernal equinox, that is on the 21st day of March, the centre of the Sun is at one of the points in which the ecliptic cuts the equator. The name 'Vernal Equinox' which is strictly applicable to the moment when the Sun's centre is at this point is often extended to the point itself. This point is also called 'The First Point of Aries' since the sign Aries is measured from it along the ecliptic. From this moment the Sun ascends above the equator, gradually getting higher and higher until at the period known as the summer solstice, which is at present on the 21st day of June, the Sun attains its maximum height. From this onwards the Sun declines again towards the equator; it reaches the autumnal equinox on the 23rd day of September, after which the centre of the Sun

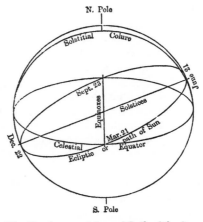

Fig. 10. Apparent Annual Path of the Sun.

passes below the equator, gradually increasing its distance from that circle, until the winter solstice is reached on the 22nd day of December, when the Sun is as much below the equator as it was above it at the summer solstice, its distance being in each case equal to the obliquity of the ecliptic. From the winter solstice the centre of the Sun again advances towards the equator, which it gains at the ensuing vernal equinox on the 21st day of March when the phenomena reappear in the same cycle.

The vernal equinox has already been defined as one of the points in which the ecliptic and the equator intersect each other. It has been found convenient for the purposes of practical astronomy to take this point as the point of reference from which the most important celestial measurements are made. There is no star actually situated so as to mark the vernal equinox, indeed the vernal equinox itself undergoes slight changes in its situation. It can however be accurately determined.

Suppose the equinox was marked by a visible point, then when that point is on the meridian of the place the sidereal clock, if correct, should shew 0 hours 0 minutes 0 seconds. The right ascension of a star is expressed then by the sidereal time at which the star passes the meridian. If, for instance, the sidereal time, at which a star passes the meridian is three hours and twenty minutes, then what we mean is that the angle between the great circle from the vernal equinox to the Pole, and the circle from the star to the Pole is three hours and twenty minutes. We may, if we please, express this angle as the intercept on the equator made between these two great circles. The length of this arc if expressed in time would be also three hours and twenty minutes, or if we choose to turn it into angular magnitude at the rate of fifteen degrees for an hour, the right ascension of the star would be fifty degrees.

§ 49. Variation in the length of the Day. The movements of the Sun will explain the familiar phenomena connected with its varying positions in the sky in summer and in winter. At midsummer, for instance, when the Sun is above the equator by its greatest amount, then of course at noon the altitude of the Sun above the horizon is equal to the altitude of the equatorial point on the meridian augmented by the obliquity of the ecliptic. This is equal, in fact, to the co-latitude of the place (that is the difference between the latitude and 90°) plus the obliquity. In this case the Sun being at its greatest altitude remains for a longer time above the horizon than at any other period during the year and we have the long days of summer. Six months later at the winter solstice, the Sun is as much below the equator as it was in the former case above. When the Sun comes to the meridian its altitude is obtained by subtracting the obliquity of the ecliptic from the co-latitude. Its meridian altitude is then a minimum, and therefore the time it remains above the horizon is less than at any other time of year. In this way we have the short days of winter.

§ 50. Arctic Day and Night. It is easy also to account for the fact that at midsummer in the Arctic regions the Sun does not set at all. For as the altitude of the Pole is equal to the latitude of the place, it follows that if at any time the distance of the Sun from

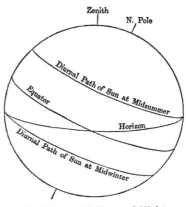

Fig. 11.   Arctic Day and Night.

the Pole be not greater than the latitude then the Sun will not set, just as we saw to be the case for the circumpolar stars. In a similar manner, we can explain how the Sun does not rise for a longer or shorter period about the time of midwinter in the Arctic regions. The actual number of days during which the Sun is invisible depends upon the latitude of the place.

As the altitude of the Pole is equal to the latitude (ϕ), the polar distance of the south point of the horizon is $180° - \phi$. If we denote the Sun's declination by D, then its north polar distance is $90° - D$. Hence, if $90° - D$ is greater than $180° - \phi$ the Sun will be below the horizon even at noon-day. At midwinter the Sun is, as we have seen, 23° 27′ below the equator or $D = -23° 27′$. Therefore, if

we put $90° + 23° 27′ = 180° - \phi$,

we have $\phi = 90° - 23° 27′ = 66° 33′$

as the latitude for which at midwinter the Sun at noon is just on the horizon, the effect of refraction being omitted (§ 54). The circle on the Earth's surface corresponding to the latitude 66° 33′ is called the *Arctic Circle*.

It is easy to shew in a similar way that on the same circle of terrestrial latitude the midsummer sun is just on the northern horizon at midnight. For the altitude of the Pole above the horizon being equal to the latitude of the place, and the Sun being by hypothesis on the horizon, we have, in this case, the latitude (ϕ) equal to the Sun's polar distance ($90° - D$). Or

$$\phi = 90° - D.$$

But at midsummer $D = +23° 27′$, hence,

$$\phi = 90° - 23° 27′ = 66° 33′,$$

that is, the same latitude as we found in the former case.

§ 51. To find the length of the Arctic Night. At any place within the Arctic Circle the latitude is greater than

66° 33', and for any given place it is easy to find the date on which the Sun ceases to rise and when it reappears. For we have only to put

$$90° - D = 180° - \phi ;$$

whence we find

$$D = \phi - 90°,$$

which gives us D, the declination of the Sun, and we can find from the Nautical Almanac the dates on which the Sun's declination has this particular value.

Thus if we take $\phi = 86° 14'$, the highest latitude ever yet reached, this simple equation gives us $D = -3° 46'$. From the Nautical Almanac we find that the Sun's declination is 3° 46' *south* on October 3 and March 11, so that if an explorer had passed the winter in this latitude he would never have seen the Sun for all that period of nearly six months from October 3 to March 11.

In a similar manner, by putting $90° - D = \phi$, we should find the date on which the Sun ceases to set even at midnight for any latitude ϕ within the Arctic Circle and could deduce the length of the continuous arctic day.

§ 52. Apparent Diameter of the Sun. These circumstances with regard to the movement of the Sun having been established we may next consider the variations in the distance of the Sun. At the first glance it appears that the Sun is sensibly of the same dimensions from one season to another. And as the apparent dimensions of an object depend upon its distance we are entitled to infer from the constancy of the Sun's apparent diameter that its distance remains sensibly uniform. But this presumption has to be modified when careful measurements are made. With the help of certain instruments we can measure the diameter of the Sun with much accuracy. We are not of course referring at this moment to the measurement of the diameter of the Sun in miles, but rather to the measurement of its angular diameter, that is to say we mean the angle which the diameter of the Sun subtends at the eye of the observer. By careful measurements of this kind it is shewn that the apparent diameter of the Sun is not constant, but that it runs through a certain cycle of changes. In winter time the apparent diameter of the Sun is greater than it is in summer.

§ 53. Apparent Track of the Sun. It is, however, obvious that the greater the distance of the Sun the less will be its apparent angular diameter. In fact we may say with a considerable degree of accuracy that the distance of the Sun and its apparent angular diameter are inversely proportional to one another. Consequently from our measurements of the Sun's diameter we are able to obtain expressions for the relative values of the Sun's distance. Thus, knowing by observation the diameter of the Sun on a number of days throughout the year, we can set down lines proportional to its distances from the Earth at the corresponding epochs. With the meridian circle we can determine the direction of the Sun just as we can that of a star. If, therefore, we take any point (F) to represent the Earth, and from it draw a line in the direction in which

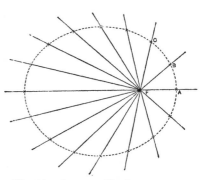

Fig. 12. Apparent Track of the Sun.

the Sun appeared on any day, and on it cut off a part inversely proportional to the measured angular diameter of the Sun on that day, and if we proceed in the same way for the other days we shall get a number of points ($A, B, C,$

etc.) representing the positions occupied by the Sun. In this way we are able to form a representation of the apparent track of the Sun. That track is obviously not a circle of which the Earth is the centre. Its form can however be entirely accounted for by the supposition that the centre of the Sun in every position lies on a well-known curve called an ellipse, the centre of the Earth being at a *focus* of the ellipse. An ellipse may be defined as the locus of a point such that the sum of its distances from two fixed points is constant. The two fixed points are then the foci of the curve. An ellipse may be very easily drawn in the following way. In a sheet of paper fix two drawing pins to represent the foci. Over these throw a loop of thread. If then a pencil be drawn round so that while writing on the paper its point keeps the loop of thread tightly stretched it will describe the important curve which is easily seen to be an ellipse according to the definition just given.

§ 54. **Effect of Refraction.** In speaking of the rising and the setting of the Sun it is always necessary to remember that the observed phenomena are largely modified by the effect of refraction. We have already explained how, owing to refraction, the apparent place of every object is pushed upwards towards the zenith. This effect is particularly marked at the horizon. And in fact the amount of refraction at the horizon is so great as to lift the Sun through an angle greater than its apparent diameter. It may be mentioned that the apparent diameter of the Sun in winter is 32′ 32″ and in midsummer 31′ 32″. So practically we may take the average value of the Sun's diameter at about thirty-two minutes. We find however that the horizontal refraction exceeds thirty-three minutes, and hence it follows that even after the Sun has completely set, from a geometrical point of view, the effect of refraction is such as to make the whole body of the Sun appear still above the horizon. Since at the eastern horizon this effect of refraction tends to accelerate the Sun's rising while at the western horizon it tends to retard his setting, we see that from sunrise to sunset there is a double reason why the Sun appears to be longer above the horizon than it would have been if the atmosphere had not possessed this refractive power.

§ 55. **Solar Day.** We have already explained what is meant by the sidereal day; it is the time required by the Earth to perform one rotation on its axis. As a matter of fact this is measured by the interval between two successive transits of a fixed star. If however we take two successive transits of the Sun, the interval between them is not the same as the interval between two successive transits of a star. For the Sun is moving relatively to the stars. If the Sun and a star came on the meridian at the same time to-day then when that star returned to the meridian to-morrow the Sun would have moved four minutes further back, so that four minutes more would have to elapse before the centre of the Sun crossed the meridian. If we take this observation day after day, we find that there is some variation in the interval by which the Sun moves back, this variation being due to the fact that the Sun's apparent movement does not take place uniformly. Sidereal time would not be adapted for the purposes of ordinary life for we must regulate our hours by the Sun. It might therefore seem natural to take as our day the interval between two successive passages of the Sun across the meridian. This interval is however not a constant one, but if we take a very great number of such intervals between two successive transits of the Sun and if we take the average of them all, we obtain what we call the mean solar day. This is the unit that is employed, for all ordinary purposes, in the measurement of time. Expressed in sidereal time the mean solar day is

24 hours 3 minutes 56·56 seconds. This mean solar day is divided into 24 hours, each hour into 60 minutes, and each minute into 60 seconds. Owing to the irregularity of the Sun's movements we do not employ the Sun itself when thinking of our measurement of time ; we rather introduce the conception of a fictitious Sun which moves uniformly in the equator. The true Sun moves in the ecliptic as we have seen, and with a varying speed, this fictitious Sun however moves in such a way that on the average its movement coincides with that of the true Sun. When this fictitious Sun, or rather its centre, crosses the meridian then a clock which is regulated to mean time should shew 0 hours, 0 minutes, 0 seconds.

§ 56. **Twilight.** The atmosphere has another effect on the distribution of sunlight which is called twilight. After the Sun has set darkness does not immediately follow. There is still a certain amount of light known as twilight which gradually passes away as the night comes on. This arises from rays of the Sun which after the Sun has set traverse the higher regions of the atmosphere and there meet with the particles which the air commonly holds in suspension. Those motes that are seen floating in a sunbeam are more or less present even at great heights in the atmosphere, and it is easy to see that the particles which intercept the light will become themselves illuminated and thus shed down that radiance which we call twilight. Twilight however ceases when the Sun has reached a certain distance below the horizon. That distance is found to be about 18 degrees. So long as the Sun is within 18 degrees of the horizon some of its light will reach us in this manner. We can thus explain the circumstance that at midsummer in our latitude there is twilight all through the night. Take, for example, a latitude of 53 degrees. Then the Pole is 53 degrees above the horizon. On Midsummer Day the distance of the Sun from the Pole is found by subtracting the obliquity of the ecliptic from 90 degrees. That distance is 66 degrees 33 minutes (§ 50). Hence it follows that at midsummer the North polar distance of the Sun must be 66 degrees 33 minutes. At midnight the Sun is of course below the horizon and will be found at a point drawn from the Pole down towards the North and continued below until a distance of 66 degrees 33 minutes from the Pole has been reached. As however the latitude is 53 degrees, this being subtracted from the Sun's polar distance shews us that the Sun must be 13 degrees 33 minutes below the horizon, but not more. We have however seen that there is twilight whenever the Sun is within 18 degrees of the horizon, and hence we see that at the latitude we have chosen there is twilight all through the night at midsummer.

§ 57. **The Sun's Motion only Apparent.** Just as it was found that the diurnal motion of the heavens was only an apparent motion and had indeed to be explained by the supposition that it was the Earth itself which rotated on its axis one way and not the celestial sphere which rotated the opposite way, so likewise we have to be prepared for a widely different explanation of the apparent movements of the Sun than that which our senses appear to suggest. It can be shewn that every circumstance connected with the apparent revolution of the Sun can be completely accounted for by supposing that the Sun is at rest, but that the Earth is revolving around it. What we actually seem to observe is an apparent displacement of the Sun with respect to the stars. But a moment's consideration will shew that such displacements do not necessarily require the Sun to be in motion, they could be accounted for by supposing that the Earth was itself in movement. Is it not plain that, if the Earth were revolving around the Sun, an observer standing on the Earth and looking towards the Sun would see the Sun projected against a part of the celestial sphere which would be continually changing? This is indeed no more than what is actually observed, and we may thus account for the apparent movement of the Sun. The fact is the observed phenomena of the Sun's movements could easily be explained on either supposition, and when we reflect that the diameter of the Sun is more than one hundred times the diameter of the Earth and that the Sun is consequently more than a million times bigger than the Earth, it seems much more reasonable to suppose that it is the Earth which moves round the Sun rather than the Sun which moves round the Earth. The accuracy of this presumption is demonstrated in numberless other ways.

CHAPTER IV.

THE MOON.

NEXT to the Sun, the most important and conspicuous of the celestial bodies, to us earth-dwellers, is the Moon. This position of distinction is not, however, due to any intrinsic superiority in point of size or brilliance on the part of the Moon itself. It is a consequence of the fact that the Moon as compared with all other celestial bodies is quite near to us—is, in fact, an attendant or satellite of the Earth revolving around the Earth at a distance of less than a quarter of a million of miles and accompanying our globe in its ceaseless revolutions round the Sun.

§ 58. The Motion of the Moon. The motion of the Moon in the heavens can easily be detected by comparing its position from hour to hour with regard to the stars near which it happens to pass. After a brief interval it will be quite plain that although the Moon partakes of the general motion of the heavens, rising, that is to say, in the east, gradually getting higher and higher in the sky till it reaches the meridian, and then slowly sinking to its setting in the west, yet it is also in motion with regard to the stars.

A careful watch will show that in 24 hours the Moon passes over about 13° of its path, and that in a period of

$27\frac{1}{3}$ days it performs a complete revolution of the heavens. This time is called the Sidereal Period of the Moon, and its accurate value is 27 days 7 hrs. 43 mins. 11·5 secs.

§ 59. **The Orbit of the Moon.** If the angular diameter of the Moon is measured carefully in various positions then it is possible to determine the path in which it moves around the Earth in a way similar to that in which the apparent orbit of the Sun is found, as explained in § 53. It is thus ascertained that the Moon describes a nearly circular orbit around the Earth, its true form being an ellipse of small eccentricity of which the centre of the Earth occupies the focus. The plane in which this movement takes place is nearly the same as that in which the Earth moves around the Sun, the two being inclined at an angle of only 5°.

§ 60. **The Phases.** We are now in a position to explain the phases of the Moon with which all are familiar. The Moon being a dark body would be totally invisible if it were not for the sunlight reflected from its surface. The Sun will, of course, illuminate only half of the Moon's surface at the same time and the extent of the lunar phase depends upon the amount of that illuminated hemisphere which we are able to see.

§ 61. **Another Moon Period.** Although the Sidereal Period of the Moon is no more than $27\frac{1}{3}$ days yet, as is well known, the interval from New Moon to New Moon or from Full to Full is $29\frac{1}{2}$ days. To explain this discrepancy it is only necessary to remark that the phases depend on the position of the Moon relatively to the Sun and that in the interval between one Full Moon and the next the Sun has moved forward in the sky. Thus, if at the time of Full Moon we note the position of the Moon with regard to the stars around it, then after an interval of $27\frac{1}{3}$ days the Moon will be found once more in the same position, but in the interval the Sun has moved on, and it requires more than two days for the Moon to make up this motion so as once more to get directly opposite to the Sun in the only position in which Full Moon can occur.

§ 62. Relation between the Sidereal and the Synodic Periods. The interval from New to New, or from Full to Full, is called the Synodic Period of the Moon, and is related to the Sidereal Period and the length of the year as follows.

If S be the number of days in the Moon's sidereal period then $\frac{1}{S}$ represents the fraction of a complete sidereal period which the Moon describes in one day.

In the same way, since there are $365\frac{1}{4}$ days in the year it follows that in one day the Sun performs the fraction $\frac{1}{365\frac{1}{4}}$ of a complete revolution (here we refer of course to the *apparent* revolution of the Sun). Hence the fraction of a complete revolution which the Moon in one day *gains* on the Sun is $\frac{1}{S} - \frac{1}{365\frac{1}{4}}$.

If we take M so that

$$\frac{1}{M} = \frac{1}{S} - \frac{1}{365\frac{1}{4}},$$

then the Moon gains the fraction $\frac{1}{M}$ of a complete revolution on the Sun each day and consequently in M days it will gain a complete revolution. That is to say, M is the number of days in the Synodic Period. In this way, if S is taken as $27\frac{1}{3}$ days we find that M is equal to $29\frac{1}{2}$ days.

§ 63. Distance, Size, and Weight of the Moon. The mean distance of the Moon from the Earth is found to be 238,800 miles. Its mean angular diameter is $31' 26''$ which at the distance of 238,800 miles corresponds to 2,160 miles. It is thus seen that the Moon's diameter is only a little

more than a quarter of that of the Earth. It would take
50 bodies each as large as the Moon to make up the volume
of the Earth. Fifty such bodies rolled into one would not,

Fig. 13. Comparative Sizes of the Earth and the Moon.

however, weigh as much. The materials of which the Moon
is composed being on the average lighter than those of the
Earth, more than 80 Moons would be required to outweigh
our globe.

§ 64. **Eclipses.** Since the Earth is an opaque body
it follows that all the rays of the Sun which fall upon it
are stopped, and consequently on the other side of the
globe from the Sun not only is the surface itself in
darkness but there is a vast region of space from which the
Earth, like a great screen, cuts off the sunlight.

If we imagine a cone described so as to envelop both
the Sun and the Earth, then the portion of space occupied
by the Earth's shadow, into which no direct ray of the Sun
can penetrate, is the part of that cone which extends
beyond the Earth on the further side from the Sun.

§ 65. **Eclipses of the Moon.** A section of such a
cone is exhibited diagrammatically in Fig. 14, in which no
attempt has been made to preserve the proper proportions
between the sizes of the bodies or their distances. From

every point within the space of which *Ptt'* is a section the Sun is wholly invisible.

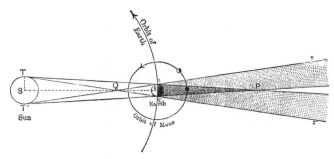

Fig. 14.   Eclipses of the Moon.

But there is another cone which is of importance in the theory of eclipses.   This is a cone with its vertex at *Q* and extending to envelop the Sun in one direction and the Earth in the other.   This cone is represented in Fig. 14 by the lines *T'Qr* and *TQr'*, and it will be seen that from every point within the lightly shaded portion of this cone the Earth cuts off more or less of the light of the Sun.   This cone of partial obscuration is called the penumbra.   We must, therefore, think of the Earth in its motion round the Sun as being always accompanied by this double cone of shadow extending out behind it into space.

The length of the shadow varies a little from time to time according to the actual distance between the Earth and the Sun but it can easily be calculated in the following way.   From the similarity of the triangles *PTS* and *PtE* we have the proportion

$$PE : PS = Et : ST,$$

and therefore

$$PE : PS - PE = Et : ST - Et.$$

But $PS - PE$ is SE, i.e. the distance of the Sun, and therefore we find

$$PE = \frac{SE \cdot Et}{ST - Et} = \frac{1}{\dfrac{ST}{Et} - 1} \times SE.$$

Now $\dfrac{ST}{Et}$ is the ratio which the diameter of the Sun bears to the diameter of the Earth and is equal to about 108; therefore PE, the length of the shadow, is about $\frac{1}{107}$th of the distance between the Earth and Sun, or on the average about 860,000 miles.

§ 66. **Lunar Eclipses.** If the motion of the Moon around the Earth took place in the plane of the ecliptic it is clear that the Moon, which revolves at a distance of about 240,000 miles, would plunge into this shadow at each revolution. If this were the case, therefore, we should have a lunar eclipse every month at the time of Full Moon.

The Moon's orbit is, however, inclined at an angle of 5° to the plane of the ecliptic. The Moon therefore sometimes passes above the shadow and sometimes below. If however at the time of Full Moon our satellite should happen to be very near the ecliptic, passing from one side of that plane to the other, then the Moon enters the shadow and is eclipsed. If the lunar globe is wholly immersed in the shadow then it is said to be totally eclipsed. If only a portion of the globe is obscured then it is said to be partially eclipsed.

§ 67. **Colour of the Moon in an Eclipse.** It should be here pointed out that if the Earth were simply a solid globe then no light whatever could penetrate into the Earth's shadow, and the Moon in a total eclipse would always be quite invisible. The Earth is, however, as we know, surrounded by a vast atmosphere and this has the effect of bending the rays which strike obliquely upon it and refracting some of them into the cone of shadow, which is accordingly not absolutely dark. In their passage through the atmosphere these rays become tinged to some extent with a reddish colour, and the consequence is that the Moon in a total eclipse is not wholly lost to sight but can generally be seen shining with a dull copper-coloured light.

§ 68. **Solar Eclipses.** In general the inclination of the Moon's orbit carries the 'New Moon' above or below the Sun as seen from the Earth. But if at the time of New Moon our satellite happens to be passing from the North to the South of the ecliptic, or from the South to the North, it may so happen that the Moon will appear directly in front of the Sun and an eclipse of the latter body will take place.

The Moon, of course, casts behind it a shadow in just the same way as we have already seen the Earth to do. We can calculate the length of this shadow, just as we did

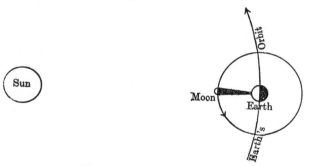

Fig. 15. Total Eclipse of Sun.

that of the Earth, from the known relation between the sizes of the Sun and Moon. Thus it is found that the average length of the shadow of the Moon when it is placed directly between the Sun and the Earth is 232,000 miles.

The average distance of the Moon from the centre of the
Earth is 238,800 miles and the semi-diameter of the Earth
is 3959 miles, so that the average distance from the Earth's
surface to the Moon is 234,800 miles.   Thus we see that
the point of the shadow would fall short of the Earth's
surface under average circumstances by about 2900 miles
But since both the length of the shadow and the distance of
the Moon vary considerably it frequently happens that the
shadow is long enough to extend to the Earth's surface, and
in that case it is clear that from all points within the patch
of darkness where the shadow falls the Sun would be invisible or totally eclipsed, while places situated within the
section of the Moon's *penumbra* enjoy the phenomenon of
a partial eclipse.

§ 69. **Annular Eclipse.**   If at the time when an
eclipse occurs the shadow does not reach as far as the
surface then it is clear that an observer situated as at *a* in
Fig. 16, will see the Moon projected against the Sun's disc
while a narrow ring of light will be visible all round it.
This is known as an 'Annular Eclipse of the Sun.'

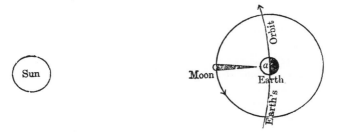

Fig. 16.   Annular Eclipse of Sun.

§ 70. **Total Eclipse of Sun.**   Of the various kinds of
eclipses which may occur by far the most important is that
known as a total eclipse of the Sun ; for when this takes

place, and the direct light from the bright photosphere is cut off, then, as has been mentioned in the last chapter, we are able to see the faint appendages of the Sun outside its photosphere which are known as the prominences and the Corona, and which at other times and under ordinary circumstances are quite invisible.

§ 71. **The Constant Face of the Moon.** The most obvious fact with regard to the appearance of our satellite arises from the circumstance that it rotates on its axis in the same time that it takes to make a complete revolution around the Earth. This is, in fact, merely another way of stating that the Moon constantly turns the same face towards the Earth.

§ 72. **The Librations.** If the Moon moved with perfect uniformity in its orbit and if the axis around which it rotates were perpendicular to the plane in which its orbit lies then we should never catch a glimpse of more than exactly one-half of the lunar surface. But in consequence of the elliptic form of its orbit the Moon moves with different speeds at different parts of its track. The motion on its axis is, however, uniform and hence we can sometimes see a little round the eastern limb and sometimes a little round the western. Also when the Moon is in that part of its orbit where the northern end of its axis inclines towards the Earth then we are enabled to see for a short distance beyond the North Pole, and when the southern end leans in our direction we see a little beyond the Southern Pole. These phenomena are called the Librations of the Moon. The glimpse of the other side is however very partial ; only 9 per cent. of the total surface is thus occasionally revealed, and even then, it is presented so obliquely to our view that but little is added to our knowledge of the lunar features.

§ 73. **Libration of the Moon.** The first of these Librations is illustrated in an exaggerated form in Fig. 17.

If *ABCD* be the orbit of the Moon around the Earth at *E*,
then *A* represents the
Moon's *Perigee* and *C*
the *Apogee*. Also, on a
date half-way between
the two positions *A* and
C the Moon's position
will be as represented
at *B*. Now if m_1 represent a mountain sup-
posed to be just at the
centre of the visible
hemisphere at *A*; when
the Moon reaches *B*,

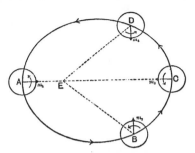

Fig. 17.   Libration of the Moon in
Longitude.

one-quarter of the whole period having elapsed, the
mountain will have made exactly one-quarter of a rotation
around the axis and will be situated as at m_2, and will no
longer occupy the centre as seen from *E*. When the Moon
gets to *C*, having made half a revolution, the mountain will
be in the position m_3 and will once more be centrally placed.
But when three-quarters of the Moon's period has elapsed
the Moon will have reached *D* while the mountain having
made three-quarters of a rotation will be at m_4 and will
again appear disturbed from its central position. This is
the Libration in Longitude.

Of what may exist on the further side of the Moon
we have absolutely no direct knowledge. But there is no
reason to think that the features it would display are
essentially different from those on the side of the Moon
which is turned towards us. Ever since the invention of
the telescope the hemisphere of our satellite which is
presented for study has been examined so closely that it
may be asserted that there is no marking on its surface as
large as Hyde Park which has not been drawn and mapped
and in most cases even had a name given to it.

§ 74. Lunar Craters. When viewed through a telescope the surface of our satellite is found to be marked in all directions by craters or rings, planes, mountain chains, and large dark patches. The accompanying figure represents a photograph of the Moon when full and shews many characteristic objects.

Among the principal volcanic remains which constitute perhaps the most interesting features on the Moon's surface we must notice the great craters Tycho and Copernicus, which are specially characterised by the systems of streaks which radiate from them. Tycho, indeed, illustrates the most perfect type of lunar mountain, although in some phases of illumination when the sunshine falls upon it obliquely, it is difficult to distinguish this particular crater among other less important craters with which the surface in its neighbourhood is pitted. As the Sun rises on Tycho, however, the preeminence of this great crater becomes unquestioned, and then the magnificent series of bright streaks appear which radiate from it in all directions and form that very striking system that can so easily be observed in a telescopic view of the Full Moon. The enormous cavity in the centre of this mountain is fifty-four miles across, while its depth is more than three miles below the summit of the ring. In the centre a rugged peak ascends to a height of about one mile. The ring is composed of four tiers of terraces on the inner side of its slope, one above the other, of an extremely steep and rugged nature.

Close to the eastern limb of the Moon is seen the well-marked plane, Grimaldi. It is remarkable for its dark colour, apparently due to some peculiarity of the soil in the interior. Nearer to the South Pole, which is the upper pole in the picture, as an astronomical telescope always inverts, lies another great plane surrounded by a mountain rampart very much foreshortened, which is known

Tycho

Mare Humorum

Grimaldi

Copernicus

Mare Imbrium

Plato

Mare Nubium

Mare Nectaris

Mare Foecunditatis

Mare Tranquillitatis

Mare Crisium

Mare Serenitatis

THE FULL MOON. Age 14 days, 8 hours.

Photographed at the Lick Observatory.

To face page 70

by the name of Schickard. The mighty wall which encloses it is more than two miles high in some parts and more than four hundred and sixty miles in circumference. A ring so vast as this is large even in comparison with the Moon's diameter, and consequently, a spectator standing in the centre might well imagine himself on a boundless plain, since owing to the rapid rounding of the Moon's surface, the ring which encompassed him would be wholly out of sight beyond his horizon.

Another interesting object is the ring known as Plato. Its great rampart is sixty miles in diameter. On the floor are found several small crater-rings, and the surface of the floor is variously coloured in irregular patches. At the south-eastern end a large mass of the ring has fallen down, forming a gigantic landslip. The surface of the Moon has been studied so carefully that a volume would be required to describe the objects which are known and of which we have mentioned a few.

We naturally ask how these appearances on the Moon are to be accounted for. Formations of the same general type are found scattered in the greatest profusion all over its surface. In these features, we find a nearly circular ring or rampart, the interior of which is generally depressed below the average level of the Moon with or without, as the case may be, a central peak. We are not without some terrestrial analogies. There are certain regions of the Earth which if seen from above under certain illumination, would present appearances very similar to those presented by these objects in the Moon. In the neighbourhood of Vesuvius, in that remarkable volcanic district, in Auvergne near the Puy de Dome, and in certain lava formations in the Sandwich Islands, we are reminded forcibly of the features of the Moon. We are thus led to attribute the numberless pits and cones which dot the face of our satellite to volcanic action. We have, it must be admitted, notwithstanding the greater scale of our Earth, nothing which can compare with the gigantic lunar Tycho with its diameter of fifty miles, and its ring of seventeen thousand feet high. As, however, we find lunar craters formed on exactly similar lines, varying in size from the smallest spots we can clearly see, up to enormous objects like those just mentioned, we are naturally led to explain the larger objects as merely the result of extreme exertions of a similar character to those which produce the smaller objects.

§ 75. Surface Characteristics. The surface of the Moon is of such a character that it would be impossible for a traveller placed upon it to make much progress in exploration without encountering tremendous difficulties owing to the peculiar nature of the lunar country. The surface of our satellite indeed displays deserts far more worthy of the name than any Saharas which our globe can produce. We need not, however, expect to find in a lunar desert the abundant sand which often characterises deserts on the Earth. The Moon seems to be a vast waste not so much of sand as of rock. Over the greater part of the lunar globe the rocky surface is so rugged and mountainous that but few regions on this Earth would bear comparison with it. But a lunar traveller would be continually beset with obstacles of a much more troublesome nature than those which confront the Alpine climber when he is scrambling over the rocks in Switzerland. The lunar surface is largely cumbered with irregular masses of rock and there would be no such facilities for getting over them as are often found on this Earth. The sharp angles of the lunar rocks have never been rounded off by the action of air and water, those two agents which have been of such conspicuous importance in the sculpture of our own globe.

There is also another class of difficulty which would greatly embarrass a traveller who set out to explore the

Moon's surface. He would frequently find his progress intercepted by a deep and wide crack of an utterly impassable character. Nor need he in general hope to accomplish his end by getting round the extremity of such a fissure. Such fissures often extend for hundreds of miles. They are sometimes intersected by other similar chasms, and these abysses are usually so deep that from our point of view we have never been able to see to the bottom of them. Owing to the distance of the Moon a fissure has to be not less than a mile in width to be distinctly visible in our telescopes. We can in fact only observe those rents which are specially prominent in the lunar surface.

§ 76. **Extinct Volcanoes.** Though I have spoken of the mighty Copernicus as a volcano, yet it must be borne in mind that this object as well as the hundreds of other similar features on the Moon are not to be regarded as volcanoes in the active sense of the word. Our satellite has been studied most carefully ever since the telescope was invented, but no observer has ever yet beheld any disturbance on its surface which could be interpreted as a volcanic eruption in actual progress. The Moon was no doubt once the seat of volcanic outbreaks of tremendous intensity, but those days have long since passed. All we now see are the remains of volcanoes which have been certainly still for hundreds of years and probably for thousands, or for aught we can tell for uncounted millions of years.

§ 77. **Sharpness of Lunar Features.** Notwithstanding the antiquity of the lunar features the observer who is privileged to look at our satellite through a good telescope will be struck with the wonderful sharpness and definiteness of outline which their details exhibit. This appearance of freshness has to be accounted for and we are able to give the explanation. The avalanches which thunder down a

Swiss mountain are in one way or another due to the
action of water which has been frozen. It may be that
the water which has penetrated into a crack in the rock,
expands in the act of passing into ice. Thus great fragments of rock are loosened, and such fragments, accompanied
it may be by great volumes of snow, break away and are
hurried down in an avalanche. This action with which
everyone who has visited the Alps is familiar, is incessantly
going forward in almost all mountainous regions. The
wearing influence of water in its various forms is ever tending to crumble away the rocks and mountains and thus to
reduce and lessen the irregularities on the Earth's surface.
In the course of ages such operations of water are constantly effecting the most remarkable transformation of the
features on the surface of the land. There can hardly be
a doubt that if the mighty crater Copernicus had been
situated on this Earth, instead of being, as it is, on the
Moon, the incessant operation of air and water would long
ago have modified the aspect of the crater from that
which it still continues to wear under the serene conditions
under which it is placed on our satellite.

§ 78. **Absence of Water.** Our telescopes shew distinctly that on the lunar world are neither seas nor ocean.
They do not indicate lakes or rivers, they do not even present
clouds or mists such as would necessarily arise if any water
were present. We have never seen a lunar mountain peak
crowned with mist and no wisp of vapour has ever been
detected in a lunar valley. Thus we conclude that the
main agent for wearing down our mountains is absent from
our satellite. And hence we need feel but little surprise
that notwithstanding the unknown ages which seem to
have elapsed since Copernicus was actually in activity,
it should still present to us with all its sharpness complete
the grand outlines of a primeval volcano.

§ 79. **Lunar Atmosphere.** The extraordinary

clearness with which the telescopic observer is enabled to
scrutinise the features of the Moon is largely due to the fact
that, unlike our Earth in this respect, our satellite is surrounded by no appreciable atmosphere. This Earth of ours
is closely wrapped around with a coat of air gradually
decreasing in density from the bottom where we live up
to about two hundred miles over our heads, where the
attenuated atmosphere is merging into open space. It has
sometimes been thought that in the lunar valleys there
may be slight traces of some gaseous body. But in any
case such covering can be no more than the merest fraction
of the bounteous atmosphere which our Earth enjoys.

§ 80. **History of the Earth-Moon System.** I
do not think there is any chapter in modern science more
remarkable than the history of the Moon which I here
propose to describe. Modern research has, however, conducted us to a glimpse of what has taken place at an
extremely early period of the Earth-Moon history—the
theory to which I now refer has been largely due to the
researches of Professor G. H. Darwin of Cambridge.

§ 81. **The Tides.** Our argument proceeds from a
simple and well-known matter. Everyone who has ever been
on the sea-shore knows that daily ebb and flow of the waters
which we call the *tides*. Long before the true nature of
the forces by which the Moon acts upon the sea was
understood it had become certainly known that there was
a connexion between the tides and the Moon. Indeed
the daily observations of a fisherman or of anyone whose
business was concerned with the great deep would have
taught him that the time of high water, at the particular
part of the coast where his business lay, and the time of
Full Moon had a certain definite relation to each other.
The fisherman might not—he certainly did not—understand
the precise influence of the Moon upon the tides. If,
however, he had noticed, as he would be likely to do, that

whenever the Moon was full the tide was high at ten o'clock in the morning, as it would be in certain ports, it would be perfectly obvious to him that the Moon had some relation to this ebbing and flowing of the ocean. The time of high water being of such importance to the daily avocations of the fisherman, the fact that when the Moon was full the hour of high water was always the same at his particular port would hardly have escaped his notice.

§ 82. **Work done by the Tides.** As the tides course backwards and forwards, sweeping to and fro vast volumes of water, it is obvious that the tides must be doing work. In fact, in some places the tides have been forced to do useful work. If the rising water be impounded in a large reservoir it can be made to turn a water-wheel as it enters, while as the reservoir empties itself a few hours later another current is produced which can be utilised in a similar manner. Thus we can produce a tidal mill. It may be quite true that it is not often possible to employ the direct power of the tides in an economical manner. It is, however, for our purpose merely necessary to note that day after day, week after week, year after year, the tides must be incessantly doing work of some kind or other.

§ 83. **Earth's Energy of Rotation.** Every practical man knows that work can only be accomplished by the expenditure of a precisely equivalent amount of what is known as energy. He knows also that there is in Nature no such operation as the creation of energy. It is just as impossible to create out of nothing the energy which would lift an ounce weight a single inch as it would be to create a loaf of bread out of nothing. If therefore the tides are doing work, and we have seen that they undoubtedly are so employed, it follows that there must be some source of energy on which the tides are able to draw. There is only one possible source for the energy necessary to sustain the tides. The Earth may be regarded as a mighty fly-wheel which contains a prodigious store of energy. That energy is however never added to, for there is no agency to impart fresh rotation to the Earth. If no energy were withdrawn from the Earth's rotation then the globe would continue for ever to spin round its axis once every twenty-four hours. As the tides need energy to get through their work, they abstract what they require from the store which they find at hand in the rotation of the Earth. It must indeed be carefully understood that although it is the attraction of the Moon drawing the water towards it on the one side, and drawing the Earth away from the water on the other side, which produces the tides, yet it is not the Moon which supplies the energy necessary for the tides to do their work. Indeed a little reflection will shew that if it were not for the rotation of the Earth relatively to the Moon there would be no rising and falling of the tide. I mean, of course, that if the Earth and the Moon rotated as one piece then the high tide would always be in the same place on the Earth, there would be no ebbing and flowing, and consequently there would be no consumption of energy by the tidal movements. It is the rotation of the Earth which causes the Earth, so to speak, to move against the tides and it is to overcome the resistance thus arising that the perennial supply of energy is demanded. This withdrawal of energy from the Earth is incessantly taking place along almost every coast. From day to day, from century to century, energy is daily being withdrawn and daily being expended but energy is never again restored to the Earth. The consequence is inevitable. The quantity of energy due to the rotation of the Earth must be gradually declining. The result at which we have arrived involves the practical consideration that the operation of the tide must be gradually reducing the speed with which the Earth rotates. The tides must, in fact, be increasing the length of the day.

This is indeed a notable consequence of those tides which ripple to and fro on our shores and which flow in and flow out of our estuaries. Owing to these tides to-day is longer than yesterday, and yesterday longer than the day before. We must however admit that the change produced is not very appreciable when only moderate periods of time are considered. Indeed the alteration in the length of the day from this cause amounts to no more than a fraction of a second in a period of a thousand years. Even within the lapse of historic time there is no recognisable change in the length of the day attributable to the action of the tide. But the importance of our argument is hardly affected by the circumstance that the rate at which the day is lengthened is a very slow one. The point which is really significant to notice is that this change is incessantly taking place and that it invariably tends to *increase* the length of the day. It is this latter circumstance which gives to the doctrine its great importance as a factor in the development of the Earth-Moon system. Astronomers are accustomed to investigate movements in the celestial bodies which advance for vast periods in one direction and then for equally long periods become reversed. Such movements as these are, however, not of the kind which produce really great effects upon the universe. Great effects do not arise if that which is done during one cycle of years is all undone during the next. The tides are, however, ever in operation and their influences tend continually in the same direction. Consequently the alteration in the length of the day is continually in progress, and in the course of illimitable ages its effects accumulate to a startling magnitude.

§ 84. **The Earth's Rotation becomes Slower.** The Earth now revolves on its axis once in twenty-four hours. There was a time, most likely it was millions of years ago, when the Earth revolved once in twenty-three hours. Earlier still it must have spun upon its axis in twenty-two hours. The very same arguments applied in those times which apply at the present, so that as we look back further and further into the excessively remote past we find the Earth spinning ever more and more rapidly, until at last we discern an epoch when the length of the day having declined to eight hours and seven hours, had at last sunk to something like five or six hours. This is the time at which it would seem that the history of the Moon may be said to have commenced, when the Earth was accomplishing about four revolutions in the same time that it now requires for a single revolution. We cannot attempt to assign the antiquity of this critical moment. It was in all probability far earlier than the time which the researches of geologists have opened out to us. If it be thought that the vagueness of our knowledge as to the length of time which these changes required is rather unsatisfactory then it must be remembered that even now historians who have human records and monuments to guide them, are still often in utter uncertainty as to the periods during which mighty empires flourished, or as to the dates at which great dynasties rose or perished.

§ 85. **Reaction on the Moon.** Among the profoundest laws of nature is that which asserts that action and reaction are equal and opposite. We have seen that the Moon is the cause of the tides. And we have further seen how the tides act as a break to check the speed with which the Earth is rotating. This is the action of the Moon upon the Earth, and let us now consider the nature of the reaction with which, in accordance with the laws of Mechanics, this action must be inevitably accompanied. The Moon, by its action on the Earth, through the medium of the tides, tends to check the speed with which the Earth is rotating on its axis, and so the Earth reacts on the Moon and compels its satellite to adopt a continuous retreat. In accordance with this action the Moon is therefore gradually receding from the Earth. It is further from the Earth to-day than it was yesterday, it will be further to-morrow than it is to-day. The process is never reversed; it never even ceases. The consequence is a continuous growth in the size of the track which the Moon has been describing around the Earth from the earliest period of its history up to the present day. It is quite true that this growth in the diameter of the Moon's orbit has been but slow, yet is not also the growth of the oak tree imperceptible from day to day, though in the lapse of centuries the tree attains a magnificent stature? The enlargement of the Moon's orbit, though imperceptible from month to month or even from century to century, has revolutionised our system in the lapse of many millions of years.

§ 86. **The Moon Retreats.** Looking back through these immense periods of time we see the Moon ever drawing nearer and nearer to the Earth. Our satellite now revolves at a distance of two hundred and forty thousand miles, but there was a time when that distance was not greater than two hundred thousand miles. There was a time millions of years ago, no doubt, when the Moon was but a hundred thousand miles away, and as we look back ever further and further to the early stages of the Earth-Moon system we see the Moon ever drawing closer and closer to our globe until at last we discern that most critical stage in Earth-Moon history, when our globe was spinning round in a period of five or six hours. Instead of revolving in a distant orbit, which has been the case ever since, the Moon was then close to the Earth, was, in fact, actually touching our globe, and the two bodies, or perhaps it would be more correct to say, the materials of which these two bodies, as we now know them, were then formed, were revolving in contact, each around the other.

§ 87. Origin of the Moon. It is impossible at this point to resist taking one step further, though in taking it we must to some extent dispense with the safe guidance of mathematical analysis which has led us up to this point. At that extremely early period the Earth was not then the solid mass which we now know so well. In those early ages it was highly heated, it was heated to such a temperature that instead of being a rigid body it was a soft molten mass of matter, and that molten globe was spinning round four times as fast as our Earth spins at present. The speed in that primitive globe seems to have been so great that a rupture took place. According to this view a part of the molten matter, comparatively small, broke away from the parent globe and formed into a small globe adjoining the greater. Thus it would seem that the Moon had its origin in a disruption of the Earth. Such is the lesson which we are taught by the movements of the tides.

CHAPTER V.

GRAVITATION.

§ 88. Kepler's Laws. The movements of the planets around the Sun are conducted in conformity with the three fundamental principles which are known as the laws of Kepler. As a first approximation it may be said that each planet moves in a circular orbit around the Sun, that each planet moves round its circle with a uniform velocity, that all these circles are in the same plane, and that each planet revolves in the same direction along its circle. When, however, more careful investigation is made it is found that the tracks of the planets are not absolutely circular. It is also found that the movements of the planets along their different orbits are not absolutely uniform. The researches of Kepler succeeded in shewing what the actual shape of a planet's track must necessarily be and also explained the law according to which the speed of the planet at each point of its path varies. The results of these famous researches are embodied in those propositions which from the name of their author are known as Kepler's Laws.

§ 89. First Law. The first of the three discoveries which lie at the basis of modern astronomy may be thus enunciated.

The path of a planet round the Sun is an Ellipse, in one focus of which the centre of the Sun is situated.

We may illustrate this by the adjoining figure. Let S be the Sun and let $ABPQ$ be the ellipse. The focus of the ellipse is well known to geometers; it is well known to the draughtsman also, inasmuch as when he proceeds to draw an ellipse by the ordinary artifice for producing the figure which we have already explained in § 53. In fig. 18 the point S represents one of the two Foci. It is not necessary to introduce the second

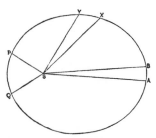

Fig. 18. The Ellipse and Kepler's Laws.

focus, for only one of the foci of the ellipse is involved in the enunciation of Kepler's laws of planetary motion. I ought indeed to say, that in the case of no one of the important planets does the actual track depart nearly so far from the circular form as does the ellipse which we have here represented. Such then is the first of Kepler's laws. But the planet as it moves round its ellipse changes its speed at different parts. When furthest from the focus which is occupied by the Sun the speed of the planet is at its lowest, while the velocity attains its maximum when the planet is passing round that end of the ellipse near which the Sun is situated.

§ 90. Second Law. The law which controls these movements was also discovered by Kepler, and has been enunciated in the second law, which may be thus stated.

The straight line drawn from the centre of the Sun to the centre of the planet moves over equal areas in equal times.

To illustrate this law with the present figure I take

6—2

two points, *A*, *B* on the track of the planet at the part
most distant from the Sun, and two other points, *P*, *Q* on
that part of the track which lies nearest to the Sun. The
planet, as I have said, is moving more rapidly in the latter
case than in the former, so that if we represent by *PQ* the
distance through which the planet has moved in a given
time at one station, and if we take *AB* to represent the
distance through which the planet has moved in a given
time at the other end of the orbit, Kepler's second law
asserts that when these times are equal the area intercepted between the two straight lines *SP*, *SQ*, and the
ellipse is equal to the area intercepted between the two
straight lines *SA*, *SP* and the ellipse. The same law
governs the changes in the planet's speed at all parts of
its orbit. So that if the area *SXY* is equal to *SAB* then
the planet will take the same time to pass from *X* to *Y* as
from *A* to *B*.

§ 91. **Third Law.** The third law of Kepler differs
from the two preceding ones inasmuch as now we compare
together the movements of the different planets. Kepler's
third law is to give precision to the fact that had been early
noticed, namely that the further a planet was from the
Sun the longer the time it took to accomplish a single
revolution. This would of course be naturally expected
from the circumstance that the larger the orbit the longer
the journey, and therefore if each of two planets were
animated with the same velocity the time required for the
greater journey would be longer than the time required for
the less. As a matter of fact, however, the more distant
planet from the Sun does not move so rapidly as does the
nearer planet. It therefore follows for a double reason
that the periodic time in the greater orbit would be longer
than the periodic time of the planet in the smaller orbit.
Kepler's third law has given precision to these inferences.
His law is enunciated in this way.

The squares of the periodic times of two planets are in the same ratio as the cubes of their mean distances from the Sun.

It should be explained that in the expression of this law we are to understand by the mean distance of the planet from the Sun a length equal to the semi-axis-major of the ellipse, which in accordance with the first law is the actual shape of the orbit. The periodic time may be expressed in the number of days and fractions of a day which the planet requires to effect a complete revolution around the Sun.

§ 92. **Illustration of Kepler's third Law.** The convenience of Kepler's third law arises from the fact that when the periodic times of the planets are known, we can deduce the relative values of their mean distances. We may illustrate the application of the law by taking the case of Venus and the Earth. The periodic time of Venus is 224·7 days, and of the Earth 365·3 days. If we divide the latter quantity into the former and take the square of the quotient we obtain the figure 0·37835. This figure therefore, according to Kepler's third law, must represent the ratio which the cube of the mean distance of Venus bears to the cube of the mean distance of the Earth. If we represent the latter by unity then this number is the cube of the mean distance of Venus expressed in the same units. But 0·37835 is the cube of 0·7233. Hence we see that the relative distances of the Earth and Venus are as 1 to 0·7233.

§ 93. **Newton's Law of Gravitation.** Kepler discovered his wonderful laws by the most diligent comparison of such observations of the planets as were available to him. These laws are monuments of ingenious and painstaking labour. But Kepler had no grounds for seeing why these laws rather than other laws should really be the guiding principles of the planetary movements. It was reserved for Newton to lay down the fundamental law of Gravitation, by which these laws were demonstrated as consequences of the principle that *every particle in the universe attracts every other particle with a force whose intensity varies directly as the product of the masses of the two particles and inversely as the square of their distance from one another.*

§ **94. First Law of Motion.** The first law of motion, as laid down by Newton, affirms that a moving body, not acted upon by any force, would for ever continue to move along uniformly in a straight line. If then a body were found to be moving in a curved line, or even while moving in a straight line if the velocity of the body was not uniform, then it was certain that some force must be in operation on that body. It was obvious that the planets move neither in straight lines nor with uniform velocities, and therefore it was certain that the planet must be acted upon by certain forces. When Kepler's laws had exhibited in the most precise manner what the actual nature of the curve which the planets pursued was, and when he had further shewn the law according to which the velocity of each planet varied at the different points of its track he had laid the foundation on which Newton subsequently developed his grand theory. Kepler having demonstrated that the planet describes equal areas around the Sun in equal times, Newton was able to shew that from this circumstance alone it was actually demonstrable that the planet must be acted upon by a force, and that the force must be always directed from the Sun. Here was indeed a remarkable advance. It was shewn that the characteristic feature which regulated the variation in the planet's velocity could be accounted for, and could only be accounted for by the supposition that the force by which the planet was controlled emanated directly from the Sun. The next question was as to the way in which the force from the Sun varied. Here mathematical calculations were possible. We can assume a certain law of force and we can shew, according to each law of force, what particular track the planet would pursue. Knowing that the track is an ellipse and that the Sun occupies the focus of that ellipse, Newton then demonstrated that the attraction of the Sun on the planet must vary inversely as the square of the distance. If the force varied according to any other law, then the orbit would not be an ellipse, or if an ellipse the Sun would not in such case lie at the focus. It thus followed from Kepler's first and second law that each planet was attracted by the Sun and that the force with which the Sun attracts the planet varies inversely as the square of the distance. This was the greatest of all Newton's achievements, described in his immortal *Principia*, in explanation of the phenomena of nature. The discovery of the law of universal attraction lies at the basis of all mathematical astronomy.

§ 95. **Second Law of Motion.** Just as the planets revolve around the Sun in obedience to this law, so the Moon describes an orbit around the Earth. This orbit is nearly circular but more accurate measurement shews that it must be regarded as an ellipse. In like manner the satellites of the other planets describe ellipses around their primaries. The memorable investigation, by which Newton shewed that the gravitation of the Moon towards the Earth was a force of the same nature as the gravitation by which the various planets are guided round the Sun, must now be explained. The first step is to shew that the force which retains the Moon in its orbit is really that same attraction of the Earth which causes a body to fall when released near its surface. Newton's second great law of motion is that the motion communicated to a body by a force acting upon it is proportional to the intensity of the force, and from this it follows that the distance through which a body will move in the first second under the action of a force is a measure of the force. It is known by experiment that a body let fall near the surface of the Earth will drop through sixteen feet in the first second. The distance of the Moon from the Earth is about sixty radii of the Earth, and as the law of Gravitation declares that the intensity of the attraction varies inversely as the square of the distance it is easy to calculate that a body let fall towards the Earth at the distance of the Moon would in each second fall towards the Earth through a distance which is found by dividing sixteen feet by 3600. It thus appears that at this distance a body will fall under gravity through about one-twentieth of an inch in the first second. If the action of the Earth's gravitation upon the Moon were to cease at any moment, then in conformity with the first law of motion the Moon would move on for ever in a straight line which would be the tangent to its orbit at the spot where the Moon was situated at the moment when the action was arrested. But in consequence of the attraction of the Earth, the Moon is compelled to swerve from the straight line and to adopt instead the nearly circular orbit in which we know that it moves. It is easy to calculate the amount by which the centre of the Moon is drawn in this way towards the Earth in the course of a second. It is found that the Moon is actually at the end of each second about one-twentieth of an inch nearer to the centre of the Earth than it would have been if the Earth's attraction had not helped it. This is precisely what the law of Gravitation would require and consequently we are assured that the force which makes a stone fall when released near the Earth's surface is precisely the same force, suitably reduced, however, in accordance with Newton's Law, which controls the monthly movement of the Moon.

§ 96. **Planetary Perturbations.** One of the most interesting applications of the principle of gravitation is to the explanation of what are known as the perturbations of the movements of the planets. The Sun is so great that it enormously exceeds in mass all the planets taken together. We may, therefore, on a first view, regard the influence of the Sun as so predominant in the Solar system that the planets move entirely in accordance with its guidance. It must however be remembered that the law of gravitation affirms that every particle in the Universe attracts every other particle. And consequently the planet Jupiter, for instance, is not alone guided in its elliptic path by the attraction of the Sun, but is affected to a certain extent by the attractions of the other planets. The Earth and Venus, Mars and Saturn, Uranus and Neptune, each exercise distinct effects upon the movements of Jupiter. The consequence of this is that although the planet has a motion which is in the main that which would be produced by the attraction of the Sun only, yet when its movements are closely looked into there are seen to be slight divergences between the simple elliptic movement that would be conducted in accordance with Kepler's laws and the actual movements which the telescope shews to belong to the planet. The theory of universal gravitation has generally reconciled the theory and the observations. Discrepancies in the calculated places of the planet, as those places would be if the motion were purely elliptic, are usually seen to agree with the calculated amounts of the disturbances which the other planets would produce.

The most illustrious mathematicians have expended their powers on the study of this great subject, and many magnificent discoveries have rewarded their labours. It has been shewn for example that although a planet does not move exactly in an ellipse, yet when long periods of time are concerned the motion of the planet may be most perfectly represented by movements in an ellipse, if we make the additional supposition that the ellipse itself is not constant in form or in position, but that it is undergoing slight changes. According to this view we always think of a planetary movement as taking place in an ellipse, but in an ellipse which is itself undergoing slow changes. Some propositions have been arrived at by mathematical research which exhibit the nature of these movements in the very simplest manner. I shall suppose for instance that we are now considering only two planets, whose mutual disturbance affects the simplicity that the orbits would otherwise possess. It was shewn by the great mathematician, Lagrange, that notwithstanding the incessant attraction of one planet on the other, and notwithstanding the many other changes which the ellipse would undergo, yet there was one very important feature in the ellipse which would undergo no change. It was shewn that the length of the axis of the ellipse would be constant. It was also proved, in the case of two large planets that though they might each affect the eccentricity of the other's orbit yet that the fluctuations of those eccentricities would be always restricted within narrow limits. It was shewn that if the orbits were once nearly circular in their form they would always remain nearly circular in their form. It was further demonstrated that though the inclinations of the orbits to each other might undergo slight changes, yet that those changes could only be slight. It should be added that these latter results are only true on the supposition that the planets revolve around the Sun in the same direction. If the directions in which the two planets revolved were different, that is to say, if one of the planets was revolving in the same direction as the hands of a clock, while the other planet was revolving in the opposite direction, then these guarantees for the stability of the system would not be given. As, however, we find the planets all do revolve in the same direction we are assured that in the case of the principal planets at least the magnitudes of their orbits, as measured by the dimensions of the principal axes, shall remain unchanged, while the eccentricities of those orbits, as well as their mutual inclinations, will only vary between very narrow limits. It need hardly be said that these propositions are of the utmost importance to a planet considered as an abode of organised life. It is obviously essential for the welfare of the inhabitants of the Earth that the Earth should remain in or about the same distance from the Sun and that the succession of its seasons should not be subject to such extreme variations as might arise if the eccentricity of the orbit, or its inclination, were seriously altered. The assurance that no important alterations can arise has been given by the labours of the great mathematicians, especially Lagrange and Laplace.

§ 97. Determination of the Mass of a Planet. We are also indebted to the principle of gravitation for our means of solving the very important problem of finding the masses of the different bodies in the solar system. In the first place it is desirable to compare the mass of the Earth with the mass of the Sun. We have already explained how the attraction of the Earth is exhibited in making a body at its surface fall 16 feet in the first second. We know, however, that the average distance of the Sun is nearly equal to 23300 radii of the Earth. If therefore the attraction of the Earth acted on a body revolving around it at this distance it would make that body fall towards it in the course of a single second through a distance which was equal to 16 feet divided by the square of 23300. But just as we were able to find the distance through which the Moon falls in towards the Earth by considering the size of the Moon's orbit and the length of the month (§ 95), so we are able to calculate the distance through which the Earth falls in one second

towards the Sun. We find in this way that the distance
through which the Earth falls towards the Sun in the
course of a single second is 324,000 times as great as the
distance through which the Earth would cause a body
revolving at the same distance to fall. Therefore the
attraction of the Sun must be 324,000 times as great as
that of the Earth. And hence, taking the mass of the
Sun as unity, we have for the mass of the Earth the
fraction $\frac{1}{324000}$.

§ 98. **Mass of a Planet with a Satellite.** In the
process of weighing a planet we must make a distinction
between those planets which are provided with attendant
satellites and those which are not so accompanied. In the
former case the problem of determining the mass of the planet
offers but little difficulty. The movements of the satellites
have been carefully examined by astronomers and thus the
distance through which the satellite falls towards the
planet in each second is easily computed. We also know
from the movement of the planet itself the distance
through which it drops towards the Sun in the course
of a second. And hence we have the simple method of
finding the ratio of the mass of the planet to the mass
of the Sun.

§ 99. **Mass of a Planet without a Satellite.** Much
more difficult is the problem of ascertaining the mass of a
planet which, like Venus or like Mercury, is not attended by
known satellites. The only method of solving the problem
in this case is to determine the perturbations in the
movements of the other planets which are produced by
the action of these bodies. The amount of perturbation
that the Earth, let us say, experiences by the action of
Venus depends on the mass of Venus, and if therefore
observations are made as to the extent to which the Earth
has been disturbed by this planet, then we have an indication of what the mass of the planet must be, by whose

attraction that particular disturbance has been caused. This method seems very elaborate, no doubt, but yet it admits of considerable accuracy. A striking verification of its utility was provided in the case of the planet Mars. Until the discovery of the satellites of this planet in 1877 our only knowledge of the mass of Mars was inferred from the perturbations which that planet caused in the movements of its neighbours. When these interesting satellites were discovered the mass of the planet was at once obtained by the simpler and more accurate method. It was, however, found that the value of the mass which was obtained from the observations of the satellites was in practical agreement with the mass which had been deduced from the perturbations.

§ 100. **Superficial Gravity.** The intensity of gravitation at the surface of a celestial body will depend of course on the mass of that body. But it will also depend on the body's density, for the less the density the greater the bulk of the body corresponding to a given mass, and consequently the greater is the distance of any particle on its surface from its centre. It is interesting to note the variations in the gravitation at the surfaces of the different bodies of the solar system. Thus, for instance, in the case of the Sun, it can be shewn that the gravitation at the surface of that great globe, is twenty-seven times as great as the gravitation of the surface of the Earth. We mean by this that if we have a mass which weighs one pound upon the Earth then to sustain its weight at the surface of the Sun would call for as much effort as would suffice to sustain a weight of twenty-seven pounds on the surface of the Earth. We may put the matter in another way. Suppose that a weight was suspended from a spring balance, and that the same weight and the same spring balance were transferred to the surface of the Sun. It would then appear that the indication of the spring balance, as given on the Earth, would only amount to one-twenty-seventh part of what the same balance would indicate on the Sun.

The mass of Jupiter is three hundred times as great as the mass of the Earth, but owing to the vast bulk of Jupiter and the low specific gravity of his materials the intensity of gravitation at the surface of the planet is not nearly so great as might be expected from his great mass ; it is indeed no more than about two and a half times as great as the gravitation on the surface of the Earth.

An instance of the opposite kind is presented by the Moon. The mass of the Moon being only about one-eightieth part of the mass of the Earth, it would be expected of course that a body should weigh less at the surface of the Moon than the same body would weigh here. On the other hand the diameter of the Moon is only about a fourth of the diameter of the Earth. The consequence is, reserving only round numbers, that the weight of a body on the Moon is only a sixth of the weight which the same body has here. A labourer could, for instance, carry six times the load on the Moon that he could carry with the same exertion on the Earth.

§ 101. Perturbations of the Moon's Orbit. Some very interesting illustrations of universal gravitation are afforded by the movements of the Moon. Just as the planets are disturbed in their movements around the Sun by the attractions of the other planets, so the movements of the Moon around the Earth are also incessantly undergoing perturbations. These perturbations of the Moon have however been produced very differently from the perturbations of the planets. We have already explained how the planets attract one another. No doubt the planets also attract the Moon, but their effect in disturbing the movements of our satellite may be considered as insensible. The disturbance of the Moon's orbit around the Earth arises from the attraction of a much more important body. It is the attraction of the Sun itself. The Moon is so close to the Earth that the attraction of the Earth is the dominating influence, and the movements of the Moon are mainly controlled by the Earth. The Sun is about four hundred times as far from us as the Moon, and consequently the attractive force of the Sun or rather its disturbing effect is greatly lessened, still owing to the large mass of the Sun its disturbance of the Moon is quite considerable, even at that distance. Many irregularities in the Moon's movements have to be attributed to the disturbing solar effect. I may mention one of them which was discovered by Tycho Brahe.

§ 102. **Annual Equation.** Let us just think of the case of Full Moon. In that phase the Moon is at the further side of the Earth from the Sun, and the attraction of the Sun on the Earth is therefore greater than its attraction on the more distant Moon. The Earth is therefore more drawn to the Sun than is the Moon and thus the distance between the Earth and the Moon is increased. At the time of the first quarter, however, the Earth and the Moon are both at practically the same distance from the Sun. They are consequently both drawn by the same force and as the disturbing force acts in lines which are very nearly parallel there is but little tendency under these circumstances to alter the distances of the two bodies. On the other hand, at New Moon the Moon is nearer the Sun than the Earth is, and consequently the Moon is more drawn towards the Sun than is the Earth, and therefore again, the tendency of the solar attraction is to increase the distance between these two bodies. Thus on the whole the tendency of the disturbing solar effect is to increase the size of the Moon's orbit. For we have seen that at New Moon and Full Moon that orbit is increased while at the first quarter and the last there is no tendency to change it.

As however the Earth is revolving around the Sun in an elliptic path the Earth is sometimes nearer the Sun than on other occasions. When the Earth is in *Perihelion,* being then nearest to the Sun, the disturbing effect on the Earth and Moon is a maximum. On the other hand, when the Earth is in *Aphelion,* then our globe being at its greatest distance from the Sun, this disturbing effect is a minimum. Now we have seen how the disturbing effect of the Sun tends to increase the size of the Moon's orbit and thus tends to increase the Moon's periodic time. We have also seen how the action of the Sun in producing this increase of the Moon's periodic time is of greater efficiency at the time of perihelion than at the time of aphelion. We have consequently a certain annual alteration. And this produces its effect in a change of the apparent place of the Moon from what that place would be if the Moon pursued its course without experiencing a solar disturbance, or if this solar disturbance acted equally at all times of the year.

§ 103. **Secular Acceleration of the Moon.** One of the most famous of the irregularities in the Moon's motion is due to what is called the secular acceleration. We have seen how the annual equation arises from the eccentricity of the Earth's orbit. As however the planets are continually acting upon the Earth they produce changes in the eccentricity. And as the eccentricity affects the annual variation, it follows that in this way the influence of the planets is propagated into the annual equation. It can also be shewn that the greater the eccentricity of the orbit of the Earth the larger is the orbit of the Moon, and *vice versâ.* Under present conditions the effect of the planetary disturbances is to cause a gradual decline from century to century in the eccentricity of the Earth's orbit. We have accordingly a correspondingly gradual decrease in the size of the Moon's orbit. And with the lessening of that orbit comes a decrease in the periodic time of the revolution of the Moon. This phenomenon has been brought to light by the comparison of the observations of ancient eclipses with the calculated movements of the Moon. About one-half of the observed acceleration of the Moon's motion can be accounted for by these planetary perturbations.

§ 104. **Precession of the Equinoxes.** We are also indebted to the theory of gravitation for the explanation of a remarkable celestial phenomenon which had been noticed ages before the cause of the phenomenon was understood. If the Earth were a perfect sphere then the attraction of any celestial body, such as the Sun or Moon, would act through the centre of that sphere, and the rotation of the body would remain unaffected. But the Earth is not a perfect sphere, it is protuberant at the Equator, and the consequence is that the attraction of the Sun and Moon on that protuberant part is responsible for certain irregularities in the position of the Earth's axis of rotation which cause what is known as the precession of the equinoxes.

The phenomenon of precession may be illustrated by the common peg top, which when set spinning will rotate about the axis of symmetry through the top itself, and under certain circumstances that axis will describe a cone with a slow motion. The axis of the Earth has a somewhat corresponding movement. While the Earth rotates rapidly around its axis once in the course of each sidereal day, the axis itself describes a slow conical movement, in consequence of which the celestial pole moves round a small circle on the sphere in a period of 25,800 years. The effect of this precessional movement of the Pole on the right ascension and declination of stars has to be taken account of by the practical astronomer. We shall describe the effect of precession on the apparent places of the stars in a later chapter.

CHAPTER VI.

MERCURY AND VENUS.

§ 105. Planets near the Sun. The several planets revolve around the Sun in the centre in orbits which in the case of the important planets are nearly circular. The orbits are represented in the accompanying figure. The

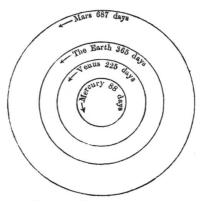

Fig. 19.   The Inner Planets.

planet nearest to the Sun is Mercury, which revolves in a period of 88 days. Then comes Venus with a period of 225 days; next follows the Earth; and then Mars with a period of 687 days; these constitute the so-called inner planets. They are succeeded by the minor planets or asteroids, after which as will be shewn later we come to the mighty planets of the system.

The innermost planet Mercury is a comparatively small object, having a diameter only three-eighths that of the Earth. This object is so close to the Sun that for by far the greater part of each revolution it is too close to the Sun to be visible. Even when Mercury is seen it cannot be studied with the same minuteness as other members of the system which are not only larger but also much better situated for telescopic scrutiny. Mercury is however frequently to be seen either immediately after sunset or directly before sunrise ; the almanac will give the proper times. But in no case is it of such interest as the other inner planets Venus and Mars, to the consideration of which we now proceed.

§ 106. Size of Venus. The Earth and the planet Venus so closely resemble each other that it is doubtful whether we know in the whole Universe of two celestial bodies so nearly identical. To begin with, the twin pair of planets are very nearly of the same size. The diameter of the earth is 7918 miles, while that of Venus is 7660 miles. We thus see that our globe is somewhat greater than Venus, but how slight is the difference in the two diameters. It amounts to no more than the thirtieth part of the whole. If a pair of billiard balls had no greater proportional difference in their sizes than the difference between Venus and the Earth it would be hardly possible to detect the difference between one ball and the other without measurement.

§ 107. Weight of Venus. As to the relative weights of the two globes, we must admit that here, to a very certain extent, we are not on very sure ground. It is not an easy matter to determine accurately the weight of the Earth, it is still more difficult to find the weight of Venus. But so far as our knowledge goes, the resemblance which the two planets shew in bulk extends also to their weight. The Earth appears to be but little heavier than Venus, in fact, in weight no less than in size, the two globes may be described as astonishingly alike.

§ 108. **Sun's Light and Heat on Venus.** As to the direct supply of heat and light from the Sun the sister planet Venus is rather more highly favoured than our Earth. It can be easily calculated that the fervour and brightness of the sunbeams falling on Venus are about double as intense as those which are received by this Earth from the same source. There is however another consideration which must here be taken into account. The period required by Venus to complete one of its revolutions around the Sun is only 225 days. It therefore follows that the seasons on the sister planet run through their changes much more rapidly than do the corresponding seasons on the Earth. The summer, for instance, would not be two-thirds the length of our summer. Perhaps, however, the extra warmth and light received by the planet would serve as a compensation, so that supposing that planet was the home of vegetation, the seed-time and the harvest could succeed each other on Venus more rapidly than is the case on our globe where the sunbeams are showered down so much more sparingly.

§ 109. **Rotation.** Considering that our Earth turns round once in twenty-four hours, thus producing, of course, the alternating day and night, it is very interesting to enquire to what extent Venus may in this respect also resemble our globe. Of course that half of the planet Venus which happens to be turned towards the Sun revels in the glory of the strong sunbeams, while the other half of the planet, necessarily averted from the Sun, experiences the gloom of night. We desire to know whether Venus rotates on its axis, and if it does under what conditions its rotations are performed. Only when these questions have been answered can we form any notion as to what may be the law of the succession of day and night on Venus, or whether, in fact, there is any such succession at a particular locality on the planet.

Astronomers have accordingly devoted much attention to the careful scrutiny of the planet with the view of discovering in what way it turns round on its axis. I may here say that the difficulties connected with this research are so great that even at this moment we cannot feel confident that they have been completely overcome. The fact is, that Venus presents to our telescope a bright and shining globe so unsullied by any conspicuous marks or spots that it is very difficult for us to study the rotation of its globe. If there were on the surface of the planet even one distinct and definite mark, which could be unmistakeably recognised in our great telescopes when the side of the planet on which it lay was properly placed, then by the study of the successive appearances of this spot, as it was brought into view by the planet's rotation, we should be able to learn how many hours the planet required to perform a revolution. But unfortunately Venus bears on its fair surface no conspicuous marks of the kind required. There are only certain very faint features which can occasionally be discerned with more or less accuracy. Our information as to the rotation of the planet is therefore derived only from somewhat unsatisfactory sources. The distinguished Italian astronomer Schiaparelli has paid particular attention to this delicate subject. The result of his enquiries is very interesting, and indeed so unexpected, that it may be said to be almost startling. He has shewn it to be highly probable that Venus conducts its movements in such a manner as always to present the same face to the Sun. Just as the movements of the Moon are so arranged that our satellite always shews the same face to the Earth, so it would now seem that Venus behaves in exactly the same manner as regards the great central luminary.

One consequence which would follow from this motion should be specially noted here in connexion with the possible existence of life on the sister planet. If the rotation of the planet be what is supposed then one hemisphere must enjoy perpetual day with the Sun for ever overhead. On such a world the phenomena of sunrise and sunset would be equally unknown. Those unhappy regions which are situated on the other side of the planet must forever endure the gloom of night. It is obvious under these circumstances that if there be life on Venus then that life must all be crowded into that one hemisphere where the sunshine is perennial. Regions on the other side of the planet would be submitted to appalling conditions of everlasting frost. Living forms would require to be considerably modified from those which we know here, ere they could be adapted to dwell in a blaze of perpetual sunbeams. If there be inhabitants on Venus endowed with curiosity and enterprise akin to that which characterises the inhabitants of our Earth, they may be occasionally tempted to despatch exploring expeditions from their sunny climes to discover the mysteries of their dark hemisphere, just as we send forth expeditions in the hope of solving the mysteries of our Arctic and Antarctic regions.

More recently however an ingenious spectroscopic method has been applied to the investigation of the rotation of Venus. Belopolski has shewn that the long period of rotation which Schiaparelli's observations seem to indicate is probably erroneous. He concludes the period must be a short one, perhaps comparable with the length of our own day. The question is still not finally settled.

Telescopic observers have always been specially struck with the extraordinary brightness of Venus. To possess such brightness it would seem that the globe, in so far as we see it, cannot be composed of materials resembling those of which our Earth's surface is formed. The only explanation that we are able to give is that Venus is probably covered by vast clouds and from the upper surface of these clouds the sunbeams are reflected. It is thus suggested that water must be present on this planet, for we do not know any material by which such clouds could be produced otherwise. Acute observers have sometimes thought that they have discerned the presence of caps of ice and snow at the poles of Venus, just as there are similar caps of ice and snow perennially at the poles of our Earth, while there are also, at the proper seasons, similar ice caps on the poles of Mars. Evidence has been collected in many ways to prove that there is an atmosphere around Venus. We cannot indeed assert that this atmosphere, either in its composition or in its abundance, has any resemblance to the atmosphere which surrounds our Earth. A gaseous envelope of some kind does however most certainly enfold this star.

CHAPTER VII.

MARS.

§ 110. Resemblance to the Earth. If Venus be like the Earth in bulk and mass the planet Mars in Physical features still more nearly resembles our globe. Indeed the study of this neighbouring planet is, from every point of view, of extreme interest.

We use the word 'neighbouring,' however, with certain modifications. Mars is certainly not the Earth's nearest neighbour. That position, of course, belongs to the Moon. And even among the planetary hosts it is known that an insignificant little asteroid named Eros comes at certain seasons much closer to our Earth than does Mars. As, however, the globe of Eros is too minute to permit us to make any detailed examination of its surface, this asteroid offers but little attraction to the astronomer when viewed merely as a telescopic object.

It must also be borne in mind that under certain conditions Venus approaches the Earth much more closely than Mars is ever permitted to do. But when Venus comes closest to our view, it happens that it is then not at all suitably placed for observation. The telescopic pictures of it are quite lacking in the fulness of detail which we would so much like to see. On the other hand, when Mars comes into the most favourable position for our inspection, though he still remains at the not inconsiderable distance of thirty-five million miles, he admits of being scrutinised with very considerable satisfaction to the observer. Mars is not, however, very frequently to be found in such a position. The distance of this planet from the Earth varies from one year to another, and consequently whenever it does so happen that Mars approaches specially near, a vigorous effort is made to utilize the occasion to the utmost. We have already indicated the special reason why this particular planet is in many ways far more attractive than any of the others. It is the most world-like of the celestial bodies that are known to us. In speaking of the Sun or of the Moon it is always the contrast between their structure and that of a globe like our own Earth that receives attention and illustration. Quite otherwise is it with respect to Mars. The many striking points in which Mars resembles the Earth then specially attract our notice. First as to the simple element of dimensions. It is true that Mars is a good deal smaller than the Earth, inasmuch as the diameter of the planet is less than half that of our globe. Still, considering that Jupiter has a diameter more than ten times as great as that of the Earth and a volume more than twelve-hundred times larger, we may naturally regard a planet like Mars as being nearly akin to us in the solar system, so far, at least, as bulk is concerned.

§ 111. Surface Markings. It is, however, in the actual details of the surface of the planet that the resemblances between this globe and our Earth are of particular interest. In this respect the observations of recent years are especially worthy of attention. There can be no doubt that pictures of our Earth, if drawn by an observer stationed on an external point, would be specially characterised by the partition of the whole globe into surfaces of land and surfaces of water, as well as by the circumstance that sea and land are alike enveloped by a vast covering of atmosphere. On the surface of Mars we can detect extensive tracts, usually of a more or less ruddy hue, which are generally believed to be continents of land, or rather what we may describe as vast deserts. These are separated from each other by dark regions, in some cases very dark, and until recent years it was always customary to regard these dark regions as indicating oceans of water. But the recent observations, especially those of Mr Percival Lowell at Flagstaff Observatory in Arizona, have, I think, now fully established that these dark regions on Mars cannot be regarded as oceans. Examined under the favourable circumstances which are found at Mr Lowell's observatory, definite marks can be discerned through these dark areas which are wholly incompatible with the supposition that such tracts are expanses of ocean. It now seems much more probable that the dark regions are places in which, owing to the presence of water, fertility has been given to the soil. The contrast between these dark tints and the ruddy hues of the other parts of the planet would be explained by admitting that the latter are deserts, devoid of vegetation or water. In fact, the whole surface of the planet seems to possess nothing that can be described as an ocean of water, or even as a sea. Water seems to be a very scarce element, and in connexion with it Mr Lowell has made some suggestions as to the probability of the existence of inhabitants of Mars which it must be admitted are borne out to some extent by the observations which he has succeeded in making (§ 116).

§ 112. **Polar Caps.** At the season when Mars makes its closest approach to the Earth there is no more interesting telescopic object in the solar system than the polar regions of that planet. The north pole or the south pole, whichever of the two may happen to be visible, is distinctly seen to be covered with a definite mass of white material. It is impossible not to believe that this white polar cap is a mass of ice or snow. If we were able to take such a bird's-eye view of our own globe as we obtain of Mars under the circumstances mentioned, we should find around the Pole an accumulation of ice and snow which would give to the neighbourhood just the same aspect as that which Mars presents to us. The evidence that these Martian caps are composed of snow becomes very much strengthened when we notice that their limits are not invariable. Sometimes the white mass, whatever it may be, advances to lower latitudes of the planet, sometimes it retreats so as to withdraw more closely to the Pole, and sometimes it vanishes altogether.

It should also be noticed that Mars has seasons of Summer and seasons of Winter. They are of course in no way related to our seasons which are designated by the same names. But in virtue of the movement of the planet around the Sun and of the inclination of its axis to the plane of its orbit, it is obvious that there must be a winter and a summer on Mars contrasted in much the same way as the seasons are here. When it is summer in the Northern hemisphere of Mars, it will be winter in the Southern hemisphere on the same globe, and *vice versâ*. Careful observations have demonstrated the significant circumstance that during the Martian summer the icy polar mass or, at all events, the *white* mass, is observed to decline and shrink, while during the winter it again enlarges and occupies once more the neighbouring regions. In some cases the retreating sheet leaves behind it fragmentary portions isolated on mountain summits, and these become reunited with the main mass when in the course of time the season of extension has again returned. Considering the analogy of our own Earth, and all the circumstances of the case, it is hardly reasonable to refuse our assent to the belief that what we are looking at must be indeed a vast cap of ice and snow covering the polar regions of the planet. If this is admitted its existence forms a very important piece of testimony in favour of the doctrine that water exists on Mars.

§ 113. **Atmosphere.** It no longer admits of any question that this planet which is already so like our Earth in the respects we have just named is also like our Earth in the possession of an atmosphere. Recent observations have left no room for doubt on this point. It must, however, be acknowledged that the atmosphere round the Earth is far more voluminous than that around Mars. Indeed it seems very doubtful whether it would be possible for an observer, looking at our Earth from the same distance at which we have to look at Mars, to be able to obtain any very clear idea as to the positions of the great oceans or the trend of the various continents. The obstruction offered by the atmosphere of our Earth is so considerable that there would be great difficulty in seeing anything clearly on its surface. It is at all events quite certain that we are able to distinguish the several features on Mars far more clearly than any inhabitant of Mars would be able to distinguish the features of our Earth. This consideration at once leads to the conclusion that the atmosphere which surrounds the ruddy planet must be much less copious than the atmosphere on our Earth, at the bottom of which we reside. Here then is an important distinction between Mars and the Earth in so far as the quantity of its atmosphere is concerned. There remains, however, a very important question as to the nature of the gases which compose the Martian air. This would of course be a vital question so far at least as the relations of the Martian inhabitants is concerned. We do not, however, possess at present any adequate information on this important matter. There is some reason to think that the gases in the atmosphere of Mars are not widely different from the gases which compose our own atmosphere. But it is very unlikely that the proportions in which the different gases are mixed should be at all similar in the two bodies.

Among many interesting observations that have been made of Mars in recent times we shall first specially notice the work of Monsieur Perrotin. He has minutely studied the atmosphere of the planet with the grand telescope at Nice in the south of France, and he has added a good many interesting facts to our knowledge.

§ 114. The Canals. Monsieur Perrotin has also secured some valuable observations which may be regarded as having finally set at rest certain points in the physical geography of Mars which have long been in dispute. It is now many years since the distinguished Italian astronomer Professor Schiaparelli announced that the continents of Mars were in many places traversed from coast to coast by long straight streaks. From the analogy suggested by their appearance he designated these objects as canals. It may illustrate the difficulty and the delicacy of such observations when we add that certain other astronomers of acknowledged skill, and provided with excellent instruments, have not succeeded in detecting these remarkable features. Perrotin, however, adds the weight of his high authority to confirm the observation of Schiaparelli. He says that although at the time he made his observation the conditions were not quite so favourable as might be desired for the examination of some of the canals, yet certain of them were wholly unmistakable, and in alluding to the controversy, he adds, that some of these were so easy to recognise that even the most prejudiced observer must have been convinced.

§ 115. Changes in the Great Syrtis. At the same observatory special pains had been given to the study of the remarkable tract on Mars which Perrotin designates as the Great Syrtis. This used to be regarded as a sea or ocean, but according to our present knowledge it should rather be regarded as a tract in which the presence of water is sufficient to render vegetation possible. Perrotin has compared together the drawings of the Great Syrtis made at different times, and it has been distinctly found that changes in the outline of this remarkable feature can be discerned. The view which Perrotin takes is that mists and clouds though prevailing on Mars in a lesser degree than they do here, are still at times sufficiently copious to obscure our view, and to hide some of the canals traversing the northern regions near the Great Syrtis.

§ 116. **Lowell's Theory.** These canals, which were discovered by Schiaparelli and whose existence was confirmed by Perrotin, have also been studied by Mr Percival Lowell. The view which he puts forward is connected with the remarkable circumstance now certainly established that there are no wide seas or oceans on Mars. Water there is on the planet, but that water is not of sufficient abundance to form great sheets such as occupy so large a part of our Earth. The consequence is that if there be inhabitants on Mars the provision of the supplies of water necessary for their welfare is a matter involving skilled organisation. Each winter of that planet sees, as I have explained, the accumulation of a cap of ice and snow around the corresponding Pole. In the course of the ensuing summer that icy mass, or at any rate a very great portion of it, is restored to the form of water. Mr Lowell has detected around the Poles of Mars what he believes to be the masses of water that have been thus accumulated.

§ 117. **Rotation.** The definiteness of the markings on Mars makes it a comparatively easy matter to determine the time in which it performs a rotation on its axis or the length of its day. In this particular, too, we find that this planet closely resembles the Earth, as it takes

only about 41 minutes longer to rotate than does the
Earth. The exact length of its day is 24 hrs. 37 mins.
$22\frac{3}{4}$ secs.

§ 118. **Satellites.** Up to the year 1877, Mars was
believed to be, like Venus, unattended by any satellites ;
but in that year, taking advantage of the fact that Mars
approached unusually close to the Earth, Prof. Asaph Hall
discovered two minute moons attending the planet.

The outer of these satellites revolves around the planet
in the period of 30 hrs. 17 mins. 54 secs. ; it is the inner
satellite which has commanded the attention and curiosity
of every astronomer in the world. The inner satellite of
Mars moves round in 7 hrs. 39 mins. 14 secs. ! It, in fact,
revolves three times round Mars in the same time that
Mars can turn round once. This circumstance is without
a parallel in the Solar System ; indeed so far as we know it
is unparalleled in the Universe. There is no other known
case where a satellite revolves around its primary more
quickly than the primary rotates on its axis.

Both of these bodies are extremely minute. Deimos,
the outer, in all probability does not exceed 18 miles in
diameter, while Phobos, the inner one, can scarcely exceed
23 miles in diameter.

CHAPTER VIII.

THE ASTEROIDS.

§ 119. Number of Asteroids. Nearly five hundred comparatively small globes which we call Asteroids are now known to belong to the solar system. The planets so designated may be described as small when we think of the robust dimensions of our Earth or even of the Moon. They would however be by no means unimportant when judged by certain other standards. The surfaces of some of the minor planets might no doubt not be large enough to contain an area greater than that of London, but on the other hand some of them would not be too small to contain the whole of Great Britain. The position of the zone of the Asteroids is indicated in Fig. 21, which shews the solar system exterior to the orbit of Mars.

§ 120. How an Asteroid is distinguished from a star. Owing to their small size and their distance from the Earth the Minor planets are almost always invisible to the unaided eye. They are only to be observed with the help of the telescope. But though the more important of the Asteroids may be quite bright enough to be readily seen by anyone who is using a good telescope, yet the observer will generally find it is by no means easy to discriminate the planet on which he wants to fix his attention from among the small stars which are so profusely strewn around the neighbouring parts of the heavens. No doubt as a matter of fact there is the profoundest difference between the actual nature of the planet and that of a star. The latter is a sun-like object, generally millions of times bigger and hundreds of millions of times brighter than the planet. But far from the Earth as the planet may be, the stars are millions of times further still. It follows from this consideration that the intrinsic splendour of the star is, when viewed from our point of view, reduced to a feeble twinkle, a twinkle so like the faint rays emitted from the planet that, so far as mere appearance goes, it would be impossible to decide by a glance through the telescope as to which was the sun-like object and which was the earth-like object. The test by which we decide between a planet and a star is to be sought in the circumstance that the planet is in motion, while the star remains fixed. We may at least regard the star as fixed in comparison with the movements of the planet which are apparently thousands of times as great. It is therefore by making an assiduous search through the heavens for the little star-like points which are in motion that the discovery of the minor planets is to be effected.

§ 121. **Photographic methods.** The astronomer is now able to avail himself of a new and greatly superior method by which the little planet can be made to betray its existence. If a photographic plate is placed in the telescope, furnished with an accurate clock-work motion which will keep it pointing to the same part of the sky, and if an exposure of an hour or so be given to the plate, then as each of the stars has not moved it will record itself as a point on the developed picture. If, however, it should have happened that a planet was situated at the time in the part of the sky which is represented on the plate, then as this object is in motion it will not form a dot like a star, it will rather manifest its presence by a streak instead of a point. In this way the examination of a plate produced by long exposure will enable the astronomer to determine whether among the numerous star-like points scattered over the part of the sky which he has been studying there should happen to lie one of these wandering planets.

§ 122. Size. Like the greater planets, the Asteroids are generally named after classical nymphs or divinities. I may, for instance, mention one of the most interesting which is known as Vesta, the name given to it when it was discovered by Olbers in the year 1807. Though Vesta is one of the most considerable of the minor planets yet viewed in the telescope it is rather a disappointing object. It is generally speaking no more than a star-like point, indeed it requires a specially excellent telescope and other favouring circumstances to shew that Vesta possesses a perceptible circular outline. In a small telescope Vesta is merely a point exhibiting no more disc than a star. The measurement of the diameter of such an object is therefore a problem of no little difficulty. It has, however, been determined by Professor E. E. Barnard who used for this purpose the great telescope of the Lick Observatory. He thus ascertained that the diameter of Vesta is 243 miles. Most of the other minor planets are much smaller than this little globe. Indeed the great majority of Asteroids are so small as to elude direct measurement altogether. We can do little more than form conjectural estimates as to their dimensions. It seems, however, pretty certain that several of these objects are so insignificant as to have a diameter of not more than ten miles.

§ 123. Zone of Minor Planets. Discovery of Eros. The Asteroids revolve in the region of the Solar System which is included between the track followed by Mars and the track followed by Jupiter (see Fig. 21, p. 119). Such is, at least, the region within which most of these objects are confined. But there are a few of the minor planets which at one part of their path come within the track of Mars and which at another part extend out to that of Jupiter. A discovery has lately been made by Witt of Berlin, of the Asteroid which bears the number 433, and to which has been given the title of Eros. This object is quite a small one and would be of no particular interest except for one circumstance. This circumstance however makes it so remarkable that it is certainly not too much to say that Eros is of greater importance in Astronomy than all the rest of the Asteroids put together. It so happens that the track of Eros lies within the tracks which the other Asteroids pursue, so much so that on certain occasions Eros approaches the Earth to a distance not exceeding thirteen million miles. This may, no doubt, seem a large figure regarded from some points of view, but judged by the scale of distances in the Solar System, it is extremely small. Setting aside the Moon which is of course merely an appendage to the Earth, it appears that Eros comes closer to the Earth than any other globe in the Universe. Venus and Mars used formerly to be spoken of as the Earth's neighbours, but now these large planets have to yield the position of being the Earth's nearest planetary neighbour to this little globe Eros, which is so insignificant in dimensions that one hundred million of them taken together would not be so large as Venus.

§ 124. **Importance of Eros.** The importance of Eros to the astronomer can hardly be overestimated. It follows from Kepler's laws, which we have explained in Chap. V., that the squares of the periodic times of the planets are proportional to the cubes of their mean distances from the Sun. We know all the periodic times accurately. This element indeed admits of being determined with extreme precision, and as we know the periodic times we can infer from this remarkable law of

Kepler the proportionate values of the mean distances. We thus know with all desirable precision the relative values of the diameter of the orbit of Venus and of the orbit of the Earth ; we know also how many times the mean distance of the Earth is contained in the mean distance of Jupiter or of Saturn or of Neptune. Not only are the relative values of the distances of these bodies thus determined, but the proportion of the size of the bodies to their distances is also involved. We thus know, for instance, the ratio which the Sun's diameter bears to the mean distance of the Earth from the Sun. Hence it follows, speaking now quite generally, that we know the relative values of the chief dimensions in the Solar System. But that knowledge is not sufficient. We further desire to know the actual values of all these magnitudes. This information will be given if we learn any one of the distances. If, for instance, we have been able to find by any direct observations the distance of the Earth from the Sun, then with the help of our known ratios we are able to find the mean distance of Venus from the Sun or the mean distance of Jupiter from the Sun. We are also able to find the value of the Sun's diameter. In like manner if observations have taught us the distance of Mars from the Earth, then by applying the same principle of Kepler we shall be enabled to ascertain the distance of Mars from the Sun and the distances of the other planets. All our accurate knowledge depends therefore on obtaining a precise determination of the distance of one object in the Solar System. This is always a problem of great difficulty. The difficulty arises from the fact that even the nearest object to us (the Moon is again excepted) is still very remote. We therefore look to the planets which come nearest to us to help in the solution of this problem. Venus, for instance, is at its closest approach when it passes directly between us and the Sun. This phenomenon—known as a Transit of Venus—is of very rare occurrence, but when it does happen it affords certain facilities for determining the distance of Venus which have been utilized for this important piece of surveying work. On other occasions the opportunity has been taken when Mars is found in its position of least distance from the Earth, and its distance has been measured. Now however the discovery of Eros has given to astronomers an object much more suited for this investigation than either Mars or Venus. The planet Eros when it comes nearest is about half the distance of Venus when nearest, and at all times Mars is at least three times as far from us as is Eros when the right moment comes. Further, the little point which Eros presents to us in the telescope is one which will admit of extremely accurate measurement. For such work the astronomer uses what is called the micrometer, and in the best known type of micrometer fine lines, which are really the lines spun by the spider, are stretched across the field of view and are mounted in frames which are moved by screws and admit of the most accurate measurements. The measurements of a little point like Eros from the adjacent points which represent stars can be made with the highest precision known in astronomical art, and from such measurements, made simultaneously at two widely separated observatories, the distance of the little planet may be deduced. We thus look to Eros as affording the means by which the scale on which the Solar System is constructed may be best determined.

§ 125. How to Determine the Distance of a Minor Planet. The adjoining figure will explain the nature of the observations which have to be made. By previous agreement between two astronomers,

Fig. 20. Distance of Eros.

situated in observatories a long distance apart, say, for instance, at Greenwich and at the Cape of Good Hope, the apparent angular distance between Eros and a neighbouring star is measured. As the stars are at what is practically an infinite distance they may be regarded as being in the same direction when viewed from Greenwich or from the Cape of Good Hope, which are represented in the figure by the letters G and C. But Eros is comparatively so close that its distance from the Earth bears quite an appreciable ratio to the distance between the two observatories. The consequence is that the place of the planet as observed from the northern observatory is distinctly different from its place viewed from the southern observatory. Thus the two base angles of the triangle whose base is the line joining the two observatories and whose vertex is at the planet are measured and then by the operations of Trigonometry the distance of the planet is calculated.

The process I have described has already been applied with some success to certain other Asteroids. But when Eros is most favourably placed it will be at least three or four times as suitable as the other Asteroids have been. We usually express these distances in terms of the Sun's distance, and therefore we may speak of Eros as giving the distance of the Sun. To the best of our present knowledge the distance of the Sun may be now represented as 92,900,000 miles. In the present state of Astronomy it ought now to be possible to determine this fundamental element with an accuracy which shall certainly be within one-thousandth part of the whole.

CHAPTER IX.

JUPITER.

THE four great outer planets of our system revolve in orbits of which the relative dimensions are shewn in the adjoining figure. Jupiter completes its revolution in 11·9

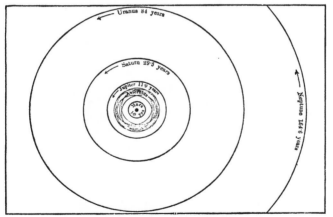

Fig. 21. The Outer Planets.

years, while Saturn, Uranus and Neptune require respectively 29·5, 84, and 164·6 years. In the present chapter we shall consider Jupiter while subsequent chapters will be devoted to the other planets.

§ 126. **Brightness.** At certain seasons the great planet whose name stands at the head of this chapter attracts the attention of every observer. On such occasions the globe of Jupiter is, with the exception of the Moon, the most effulgent object in the sky; no star can compare with it in brilliance, though no doubt the brightness of Venus at sunset will on certain occasions actually transcend any lustre ever possessed by Jupiter. Fortunately a mighty instrument is not indispensable for making some examination of the wonders of the greatest of the planets. A small telescope which can be held in the hand would suffice to shew many remarkable features on the globe. Indeed, even with no greater power than that afforded by a common opera-glass, the belts of Jupiter may frequently be seen as well as the beautiful system of Moons by which he is accompanied.

§ 127. **Equatorial Protuberance.** The adjoining pictures give a general notion of the vast planet as viewed under favourable circumstances with adequate instrumental power. In the first place it will be noticed that the disc of the planet is clearly not circular. Even a hasty examination, not to mention a careful measurement, shews that the equatorial portions of the surface of the planet are bulged outwards. There is, as we have already seen, a similar phenomenon in the case of the Earth. It is, however, there manifested on a very much smaller scale than in the case of Jupiter. Nor is it difficult to find an explanation of this circumstance. It is quite certain that a planet is made to bulge at the equator by the rotation with which it is animated, and the more rapidly the surface is carried round the more powerful is the force which tends to distort the body of the planet from the spherical form and to cause an equatorial protuberance. Jupiter turns

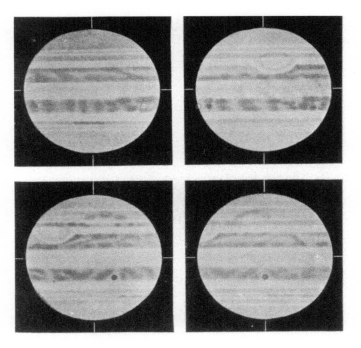

JUPITER, 1897

FAUTH

To face page 120

round on his axis with amazing rapidity when the size of his mighty globe is taken into consideration. The time that he requires for each rotation is only about ten hours. This may naturally be contrasted with the period of almost twenty-four hours which our Earth requires for the same purpose. If it be further remembered that the diameter of Jupiter is about ten times that of the Earth, it will be obvious that the strain arising from the centrifugal force on the equatorial regions of Jupiter must be greatly in excess of the analogous strain on the Earth. We need therefore no longer feel any surprise that the great planet should exhibit in such a striking manner its departure from a circular outline.

§ 128. **Belts.** The chief features to be observed on the disc of Jupiter are the remarkable dark belts which encircle the planet parallel to its equator, and they merit special attention because they exhibit a state of things unlike what is found elsewhere in the Solar System. A little careful observation will shew that these belts are not constant in appearance, they are sometimes much more amply developed than at other times. Sometimes they change their places or become broken up, while on rare occasions they disappear altogether.

§ 129. **Changes in the Appearance of the Belts.** A considerable proportion of the changes noticed may of course be attributed to the rotation of the planet. For as we have already mentioned, this body completes a rotation in about ten hours. It therefore follows that after a period of five hours the planet will have turned through half a revolution, and a complete transformation will have been effected in the hemispheres presented for our inspection. In other words, if the astronomer looks at Jupiter at eight o'clock in the evening, and turns his telescope to the planet again at one o'clock in the course of the same night, there is not a single part of the surface which was visible to him

on the first occasion within view on the second. Of course
this causes much change in the appearance of any feature
on Jupiter due to the varied foreshortening that it undergoes. But when full allowance has been made for all
variations in the attitude of the planet which arise from
its rotation it still remains perfectly certain that all the
changes in the belts cannot be thus accounted for. It is
certain that these belts cannot be regarded as permanent
settled features of the globe. If this were the case, then
by waiting for ten hours, or for any entire number of the
periods of rotation, we should always find that the face of
the planet turned towards us was marked in exactly the
same way. But nothing of the kind is found to take place.
There are sometimes changes sufficiently marked to be
perceptible in the course of even a single rotation of the
globe. It is thus plain that the belts and similar features
on Jupiter cannot be permanent objects engraved on his
mighty sphere; they must be counted as comparatively
transient and unstable.

§ 130. Clouds. A glance at the clouds in our own
atmosphere suggests at once what is indeed the true
solution of the varied appearances presented by the great
planet. It is obvious that Jupiter must be enveloped in
clouds, and it is these clouds which are presented to us
when we look at the planet through our telescopes. The
characteristic features of the planet can be accounted for
on this supposition, and here we are assisted by further
analogies suggested by our own atmosphere. The fact that
the Jovian clouds are mainly arranged in belts parallel to
the equator of the planet calls to mind at once the
analogous manner in which we find cloud belts on the
Earth parallel to the terrestrial equator. The trade winds
are well known to be connected with these equatorial zones
and to determine the positions of corresponding zones of
cloud upon the Earth. It seems not improbable that our

globe would present to an observer who was viewing it from some distance in space an aspect somewhat similar to that which Jupiter presents to us, in so far at least as the disposition of clouds on its surface is concerned.

§ 131. **Impenetrability of the Clouds.** It is, however, to be noticed that the clouds on the great planet are much more copious than are the clouds on the Earth. I do not now mean merely that because Jupiter has an area more than a hundred times as great as that of the Earth, therefore the quantity of clouds which encompass him is correspondingly larger. The cloud masses on Jupiter are indeed far greater than in this numerical proportion. Area for area, Jupiter is covered by cloud masses many times thicker and deeper than the clouds on the Earth. We can prove this by the simple consideration that our clouds, though doubtless, as we may think, often thick enough, are still not always present. They do now and then disperse, and enable us to obtain a view of the Sun. If, however, there should be any inhabitants on Jupiter they can never be so fortunate. So vast is the depth of the mighty Jovian clouds that they never disperse sufficiently to allow the gaze of one situated on the surface below them to pierce through to outer space. Nor, on the other hand, will the clouds on Jupiter permit us, who are studying the globe from the outside, to explore the depths of that Jovian atmosphere and see what its interior globe is like. It may indeed be said that we have never yet certainly had a view of any permanent feature whatever on the great planet, with one possible exception in the famous red spot.

§ 132. **Storms.** From the size of the clouds on Jupiter, and the rapidity of the changes they execute, it is manifest that the surface of the great globe must be not unfrequently swept by storms and tempests. The terrific vehemence of these changes could never be accounted for if we merely invoked the same agents for their production which are so effective in our terrestrial storms. For just see how the matter stands. The gales with which our terrestrial atmosphere is occasionally distracted are ultimately due to the action of the sunbeams by which those winds are raised. But Jupiter is five times as far as the Earth is from the Sun. The intensity of the solar heat that we receive here has therefore to be reduced in the proportion of 25 to 1, if we would learn what the intensity of solar heat is like on the surface of Jupiter. If the intensity of sunbeams were reduced to the twenty-fifth part of what it is at present, it could hardly be an adequate cause for the production of vast tempests on the Earth. We are therefore obliged to look for some other agent than sun heat for an explanation of those storms by which the surface of Jupiter is so frequently distracted. This leads to the consideration of a very instructive point in connexion with the physical conditions at present prevailing on Jupiter. It seems now certain that although the planet receives no more than a comparatively small share of sunbeams, yet that from some source other than the Sun it is provided with a supply of heat abundantly adequate for the generation of mighty atmospheric disturbances.

§ 133. **Internal Heat.** All evidence points to the fact that the internal parts of the great planet which we are now considering must be in a highly heated condition. It is indeed probable that Jupiter is so hot that, even if there was a solid surface beneath that cloud-laden atmosphere, water could not rest upon it. It would seem that the temperature is such that water would boil away from that surface, and be driven off into vapour. Let us imagine, for the sake of illustration, that this Earth of ours were to become so hot that even at the surface it was about the temperature of boiling water, and was doubtless much hotter still in the interior. Imagine the floor at the bottom of the sea to become similarly heated and to be supplied with practically unlimited heat from beneath. Then it is plain that all the water in every river and every ocean would be evaporated and turned into steam, and ascending into the atmosphere would form a stupendous mass of dense and impenetrable clouds. There can hardly be a doubt that something of this kind represents the present state of Jupiter. The constant passage of heat from the interior of the planet to its surface maintains enormous masses of material in the form of clouds in this atmosphere, while local inequalities in the transfer of this heat generate such disturbances that the incessant storms with which the mighty planet is distracted can be accounted for.

§ 134. The Future of Jupiter. It seems probable that there was a time when this Earth was highly heated in the manner just supposed. There was a time when water could not rest upon this globe in a liquid form, so that just as the present condition of Jupiter illustrates an earlier stage in the Earth's history, so the present state of the Earth may perhaps foreshadow the remote future which awaits the greatest planet of our system, when in the fulness of time it shall also have parted with its redundant heat and when the materials of its future ocean at present forming its mighty clouds of vapour shall have been collected upon its surface.

§ 135. Satellites. The astronomical student who has become possessed of a telescope is always specially interested in the beautiful system of Moons attending Jupiter. He is delighted at their incessant changes, he observes them night after night as they move from one side of the great planet to the other, he looks out for their eclipses in which the light is cut off from them, because they have plunged into the shadow which the vast globe casts out behind it into space. He watches for their reappearance at the expected moment. If he has a good telescope he will occasionally be so fortunate as to observe the satellite in the act of transit across the surface of the planet ; he will note the delicate beauty of the shadow cast by the satellite and he will follow its movement over the bright surface. He will also sometimes be able to witness the occultation of one of these little moons, as it retires behind the mighty globe, in due course reappearing on the other side.

Fig. 22 shews Jupiter and the orbits of his four satellites. The planet and each of the satellites is accompanied by an enormously long shadow. The innermost satellite (I) is shewn in transit over the disc at *a*, its long shadow lying clear of the planet. The second (II) appears from the earth to

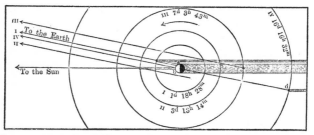

Fig. 22.   Transits, Eclipses, and Occultations of Jupiter's Satellites.

be clear of the planet, but it is casting a shadow upon the disc at *b*. The third satellite is represented as undergoing an eclipse in the shadow of the planet at *c*, while IV, though clear of the shadow, is still invisible from the earth being occulted by the planet, as represented at *d*.

§ 136.   The Fifth Satellite.   For nearly three centuries the satellites of Jupiter have received the unremitting attention of astronomers, and a fresh interest has now been created with regard to them in consequence of the remarkable discovery made by Professor Barnard in September, 1892. The four well-known satellites are all about the same size, and are all about the same apparent brightness. A telescope which can shew any one of them is generally competent to shew all four when other circumstances are suitable. The satellites of Jupiter form what are called "easy objects" in the astronomer's vocabulary. For as already mentioned, the very smallest telescopic power will suffice to shew them. Instances have indeed been recorded in which some of the satellites of Jupiter have been actually seen with the unaided eye. No doubt such observations have been very exceptional, and it suffices to mention that no one ever discovered these little objects until Galileo turned the newly made telescope upon them. None of the keen eyes of antiquity in the days before telescopes were invented ever succeeded in establishing the existence of these little objects.

It was however reserved for Professor Barnard to astonish the astronomical world with the announcement that the four satellites of Jupiter had an extremely faint companion in their wanderings. This little body is indeed so small that just as the older satellites are the very easiest of telescopic objects, so the new satellite is one of the most difficult. Only two or three of the most potent telescopes have as yet sufficed to disclose it, only two or three of the most experienced and keen-eyed astronomers have as yet observed it. The minuteness of the object will explain the difficulty of the observation. It has been estimated that if Jupiter were himself represented by a cocoanut his tiny satellite would be about as large as a grain of mustard seed on the same scale. It is a matter of but little wonder that the satellite has hitherto succeeded in eluding all telescopes save those of the most powerful description.

§ 137. **Size and Weight of Jupiter.** Much yet remains to be learned about this vast planet, which is so large that it would take no fewer than thirteen hundred globes each as large as the earth all rolled into one to equal it in size. There is, however, another very interesting line of reasoning by which we can shew how the apparent size of Jupiter is largely due to the fact that its globe is surrounded by mighty masses of clouds. Among the great problems which astronomers can solve in their efforts to measure the various celestial magnitudes, not the least remarkable is the determination of the actual masses of the planets. By the help of its satellites we have been able to discover the actual weight of this great planet Jupiter. No doubt we might reasonably expect that the weight of Jupiter should be stupendous and so it assuredly is. There is no use in trying to express it in tons, we can give a notion of the weight of Jupiter much more usefully by comparing it with the weight of our own Earth. It has been found, as might have been expected, that the mightiest of the planets is much heavier than the Earth. Indeed it weighs about three hundred times as much. But the real wonder seems to be not that Jupiter is so heavy, but that it is not a great deal heavier. Estimated by volume the planet is thirteen hundred times as big as the Earth, yet now we find that when tested by weight it has no more than three hundred times the mass of the Earth. In these figures we see at once evidence of a great contrast between the actual structure of the two globes. If Jupiter had been built of the same materials as the Earth, and if those materials were in the same physical condition, then we should expect that as Jupiter was thirteen hundred times as big, so it should also be thirteen hundred times as heavy. When therefore we find so great a disparity between the weight of Jupiter and its bigness we may feel assured that there must be some very radical difference between its constitution and the constitution of the Earth. The clouds with which Jupiter is thickly encompassed will of course suggest a method of accounting for the discrepancy. The fact is that the Jupiter which we measure is enormously swollen by the abundance of the clouds with which it is enfolded. It is these clouds which give to Jupiter a bulk altogether out of proportion to its weight.

CHAPTER X.

SATURN.

So far as mere greatness is concerned Saturn has to take the second place among the planets. The neighbouring planet Jupiter has a volume which is twice as large. Nor does the globe of Saturn offer much attraction to an astronomer. It does not present for our examination a beautiful system of continents with canals and Arctic snows, like those which are displayed on Mars. Indeed Saturn exhibits no details on his globe except a few bands which are but ill-defined, and certain marks which, though very faint, have fortunately been sufficiently recognisable to be followed during the planet's rotation. We give in the Frontispiece a reproduction of a beautiful drawing of Saturn by Prof. E. E. Barnard.

§ 138. **The System of Rings.** The feature which makes Saturn peerless among all the bodies in the Universe is presented in the exquisite system of rings by which he is surrounded. We have first to realise the dimensions of the objects at which we are looking. The outermost ring is about a hundred and seventy thousand miles in diameter. How great this really is will be understood if we reflect that the magnitude just stated is more than twenty times the diameter of the Earth. The thinness of the rings is also a characteristic which merits special notice. Under certain circumstances it will happen that the ring is turned edgewise towards the observer. In this case it requires a powerful telescope to render it visible.

§ 139. **The Structure of the Rings.** The first question which is suggested in the study of the ring system concerns its relation to the central globe. It has first to be noticed that the rings are not attached to the globe by any physical structure. They are in fact poised round the globe quite freely and the globe stands majestically in the centre of the circle which forms the inner margin of the inner ring. At first it seems difficult to imagine by what contrivance the ring remains continually balanced in the same position. How is it that the ring and the globe remain associated together during their revolutions around the Sun without ever being displaced from their relative positions? This we shall consider when we have explained the discovery which has shewn the nature of the rings. The main portion of the ring is divided into an outer and an inner part by a dark line which bears the name of Cassini's Division. This line is known to be an open space and through it the actual globe of the planet has been sometimes seen. The outer of the two rings thus separated is itself divided into two parts, by a line more difficult to see than Cassini's line. Both of these lines may be described as circles, the centre of each being at the centre of Saturn. This outer line is however not quite dark, so that it is clear it cannot be regarded as an absolute line of separation between two portions of the ring. It also appears that besides these lines which have been referred to there are certain other faint lines which become discernible under exceptionally favourable conditions.

§ 140. **"The Crape-Ring."** But the most delicate part of the Saturnian system is clearly the so-called "crape-ring." This exquisite structure extends from the inner edge of the bright ring about half-way in towards the globe of the planet. It is called the "crape-ring" because it possesses the semi-transparency of such a fabric as crape. The proof of the partial transparency of the crape-ring is afforded occasionally when the edge of the solid globe of the planet can be seen right through this part of the ring.

§ 141. **A Simple Model of the Saturnian System.** We may conveniently represent the rings in this way. Take a little globe, three inches in diameter, to represent Saturn, then on a thin piece of card make two concentric circles, of which the outer has a diameter of seven inches and the inner a diameter of six inches. Cut out this ring, it will represent the outer ring of the planet. The inner ring may be similarly illustrated by two circles of five and three-quarter and four and one-quarter inches in diameter respectively. If we now place the latter of these rings in the centre of the former and the globe representing Saturn symmetrically in the central aperture, we shall have a model of the principal parts of the Saturnian system which may render the explanation which is to follow more readily intelligible. The crape-ring is interior to the two rings already mentioned.

§ 142. **Stability of the Rings.** Ever since the days of Newton it has been found necessary to reconcile the observed facts of Astronomy with the law of universal Gravitation. It was, therefore, essential to explain how each of the rings of Saturn could remain thus accurately balanced with the globe itself in the centre. At a first glance nothing might have seemed easier. If the globe of Saturn lay exactly in the middle of the ring, as the planet pulls the ring equally all round and as the position is one of perfect symmetry the various pulls would neutralise each other, and thus the Saturnian system would be an enduring one. A little further reflection, however, shews that this simple explanation would not answer. Saturn could no more lie balanced perfectly in the middle of its ring than an egg could stand balanced on one end. The position is in both cases one of unstable equilibrium. It is an equilibrium which Nature does not like. It is therefore impossible to meet the claims of universal gravitation by saying that the ring of Saturn stands poised symmetrically round the central globe.

§ 143. **Mechanical Condition.** The appearance of the Saturnian rings in the telescope certainly suggests that they are formed from sheets of some solid material. But a few considerations can easily be adduced to shew the insuperable mechanical difficulties which attend such a supposition. It will be obvious that we may think of the ring as formed of two semi-circular arches placed together base to base. We may consequently apply the well-known mechanical principle which governs the construction of the arch to throw some light upon the question as to whether the rings of Saturn can be composed of solid material.

§ 144. **Pressure of an Arch.** I do not suppose that in any arch as yet constructed by man with the building materials at his disposal the utmost possible span has ever yet been reached. It may well be that, with certain kinds of stone, arches considerably wider than the beautiful Grosvenor Bridge which spans the Dee at Chester could be constructed ; it is however quite certain that though engineers may not heretofore have had occasion to erect the largest possible arches, yet there must be a well-defined limit which no arch can transcend. The greater the span the greater is the crushing pressure to which the stones of the bridge are subjected. The stone has of course but a limited capacity for resistance to pressure and this consideration determines the size of the largest possible arch.

§ 145. **The Rings are not Solid.** But in the

outer ring of Saturn, or rather in one half of that ring, we have an arch of gigantic span amounting indeed to considerably more than one hundred thousand miles. If this arch were indeed formed of solid material the elements employed in its construction would be subjected to pressure thousands of times greater than the pressures which could possibly be withstood by any materials such as those of which the Solar System is constructed. It must be remembered that the pressure which would prove fatal to the stability of the terrestrial arch, if that arch exceeded a certain span, arises from the weight of the materials of which the bridge itself is built. The magnitude of the pressures on the Saturnian arch would be such that even if it had been built from materials a thousand times tougher than the toughest steel a collapse would be inevitable. We are therefore led to examine how the intensity of the pressure might be reduced, and there is one obvious method by which at all events some alleviation could be effected. If the ring were endowed with a movement of rotation round the centre of the planet the centrifugal force with which its parts tend to fly outwards would of course, to a certain extent, neutralise the pull exerted inwards by the attraction of the planet. If indeed the ring were very narrow, as narrow as we know it is thin, it is conceivable that such a velocity of rotation might be communicated as would just counteract the effect of the attraction. The pressure on the materials would thus be reduced, and so far as our present argument is concerned, there would be no difficulty in conceiving how a ring, notwithstanding its many thousand miles in diameter, might be sustained around Saturn in the centre. But of course the ring of Saturn has a width many times greater than we have supposed. If that ring were indeed a plate of solid material it would require, in order to equilibrate the strain at its outer margin, to revolve in one particular period, and in a different period if the strain were to be abated on the inner margin. Even if the ring rotated with an average velocity, which might have the effect of neutralising the pressure in the middle of the ring, the pressure would be still great enough to crush the inner parts while the outer parts would be rent asunder. These are, however, only some of the difficulties which follow on the supposition that the rings of Saturn are really the solid objects which they seem to be.

§ 146. **Dynamical Theory.** The pen of the mathematician has here proved a more subtle instrument than the telescope of the astronomer for investigating the texture of the rings of Saturn—Roche first shewed, what Maxwell afterwards proved independently, that it was impossible for either the outer ring or the inner ring to be a solid object. It further appeared that there were conclusive dynamical arguments against the belief that the rings we see are composed of a myriad of thin concentric rings each formed of solid material. The analysis also demonstrated that the rings could not be composed of fluid materials. It was finally demonstrated that the only conceivable mechanical condition in which the matter constituting the rings of Saturn could exist would be in the form of myriads of comparatively small independent objects, each revolving like a moon round Saturn in an orbit of its own and each with its proper periodic time. In order to account for the apparent continuity which the rings present, as seen in the telescope, it was only necessary to suppose that these little bodies were sufficiently numerous and sufficiently close together to form a sort of swarm whose collective light would give the appearance of a continuous object, though the several individuals of the swarm could not be separately discerned. The precise size of these objects is immaterial. They might be no larger than the motes in the sunbeam or than the grains of sand on the seashore, they might be as large as mountains or even larger still, the essential point is, however, that whatever their dimensions may be, those dimensions are small relatively to the breadth of Saturn's rings.

§ 147. **The Rings are Composed of Small Particles.** It thus came to pass that astronomers received as an accepted doctrine the theory that the rings of Saturn must really be formed of small particles, moving round the planet in their several paths. Nor was this belief diminished appreciably by the reflection that visual confirmation of the fact seemed quite beyond all possibility of realisation.

§ 148. **Keeler's Observations.** Great then was the interest excited among all engaged in the study of the heavens by the announcement of certain remarkable astronomical observations by Professor Keeler with the aid of the spectroscope upon the velocity with which different parts of the ring revolve around the planet. He has demonstrated in a manner alike ingenious and convincing that the rings of Saturn have as a matter of observed fact that precise character which the beautiful dynamical theory attributed to them. Sir William Huggins some time ago made the remarkable statement that of all the discoveries in the celestial regions which the spectroscope had been the means of giving us, perhaps the most important would ultimately be found to be the revelation of particular movements which successfully elude all other means of detection. The facts already brought to light have certainly corroborated these statements, and now the astonishing announcement made by Professor Keeler, as to what he has found in the rings of Saturn, carry the doctrine a very long way towards complete demonstration.

§ 149. **The Spectroscopic Method of Observation.** The essential feature of the spectroscopic method of research which is leading to such a great extension of our knowledge can be easily described. The light from a celestial object, when submitted to examination by the spectroscope, presents a system of lines characteristic of the peculiar nature of the light which that object dispenses. If, however, it should happen that the object is travelling rapidly towards the observer, then the system of lines is shifted in one direction while, if the object be receding from the observer, the lines are shifted in the opposite direction. By measuring the amount through which these lines are shifted, it is possible to determine the actual speed at which the body is moving along the line of sight. The significance of the results thus obtained arises from different causes. In the first place, the movements along the line of sight are precisely those particular movements which entirely elude all observations made in the ordinary manner. The fact that a star is hurrying towards us, or from us, does not produce any apparent change in its place on the heavens, and yet it is only by alterations in the star's place that movements could be determined by those methods which alone were available to astronomers before the newer method came into use. The remoteness of the object is also immaterial, so far as the spectroscopic method is concerned. The process is equally available for studying the movement of a planet in our system, or of a star which is at a distance millions of times greater than are any of the planets. Nor does it matter either how small may be the object from which the light comes, for so long as that light is perceptible in the spectroscope, the dimensions of its source do not concern us. Professor Keeler has applied this method with singular practical skill to the study of the rings of Saturn. He has thus shewn that the theory of their constitution which mathematicians announced so many years before is actually borne out by observation. The sunlight reflected from the rings of Saturn is affected by the movements of the little particles of which those rings are composed; these movements produce such alterations in the position of the lines of the spectrum that it has been found possible to determine the pace at which the different parts of Saturn's rings are moving. It has thus been rendered absolutely certain that the rings consist of innumerable myriads of small particles, each pursuing its own course as an independent little moon.

Astronomers look with much admiration upon this remarkable confirmation of a purely theoretical deduction.

§ 150. Satellites. The strange and beautiful system of rings which surround this planet has occupied us so long that we have but little space left to devote to the remarkable retinue of satellites by which it is also attended. In this respect, however, it is by far the richest of all the planets. The largest of these satellites, Titan, was discovered by Huyghens as early as 1655, and by the end of the seventeenth century four more, Iapetus, Rhea, Dione and Tethys, had been discovered. Sir William Herschel added two, Mimas and Enceladus, to the list. In 1848 Bond in America, and Lassell in England, independently discovered an eighth which was called Hyperion, and so the list remained for half a century. Last year, however, a ninth was discovered by Prof. W. H. Pickering by comparing two photographs of Saturn and his surroundings which had been taken at Arequipa in Peru on August 16th and 18th respectively.

The following is a list of these bodies with the dates of their discovery and the times in which they perform their revolutions around the primary. They all move in very nearly circular orbits which lie as nearly as possible in the plane of the rings, with the exception of the orbit of Iapetus which is inclined at an angle of about 10° to that plane, and possibly that of the ninth whose motion has not yet been fully determined.

THE SATELLITES OF SATURN.

	Discovered	Periodic Time		
		days	hrs.	mins.
Mimas	1789	0	22	36
Enceladus	1789	1	8	53
Tethys	1684	1	21	18
Dione	1684	2	17	41
Rhea	1672	4	12	25
Titan	1655	13	22	41
Hyperion	1848	21	6	35
Iapetus	1671	79	7	47
Pickering's Satellite	1899	400 ?		

CHAPTER XI.

§ 151. The discovery of Uranus. The five older planets have been known since prehistoric times. There was, in fact, no record whatever of the discovery of any of the planets when on March 13th, 1781, William Herschel, who then occupied the position of Organist at the Octagon Chapel at Bath, made one of the greatest discoveries in the annals of Science. He had constructed with his own hands a reflecting telescope. This instrument possessed considerable optical perfection, so much so that when on the night in question he was examining with its help the stars in the constellation Gemini, and using considerable magnifying power, his attention was arrested by a point which did not present the appearance of an ordinary star. It had a diameter of appreciable dimensions. The perception of this fact shewed at once Herschel's skill as an observer, as well as the perfection of his home-made instrument. This will be evident when what was subsequently ascertained is borne in mind. It appeared that previous astronomers had on no fewer than seventeen occasions observed this object, but having noticed no difference between it and an ordinary star had paid it no further attention. The penetrating glance of Herschel at once perceived a difference. He looked at this object again and again ; he found that unlike a star, as to its appearance, it was also unlike in the fact that it was in motion, and ere long it was discovered that this was a splendid planet revolving outside the orbit of Saturn. This new object like the older planets revolved in a nearly circular orbit around the Sun and moved in a plane but little inclined to the plane of the ecliptic. Subsequent observation shewed that it was attended by four satellites, very small objects only to be discerned with much difficulty. The planet received the name of Uranus. Its diameter is four times as great as that of the Earth and it weighs about fifteen times as much.

§ 152. **Earlier observations.** On search being made through earlier star catalogues it was found that Uranus had been observed in 1690, in 1712, in 1715, and in 1756. On all these occasions the planet had been regarded as a star and its place had been duly set down. When, however, Uranus became known by Herschel's discovery it was possible to calculate the position which it held in the heavens on these earlier dates, and thus the identity of the planet with the supposed stars was established. If confirmation were wanted it was found in the fact that on subsequent comparison of the star catalogues with the heavens it was found that no stars were visible in the places referred to. The planet had been there seen and its place had been set down, but of course the planet then moved away and left its place vacant.

§ 153. **Discrepancies in the Motion of Uranus.** These early observations of Uranus proved however to be of the greatest importance, inasmuch as they enabled the track which Uranus follows through the heavens to be determined with much accuracy. For each revolution Uranus requires no less than 84 years, and consequently it would be impossible to determine its orbit with any very high degree of precision by a few observations separated by short intervals. When, however, the planet had been under observation for some time its orbit was accurately determined. It was also possible to determine the orbit of Uranus by means of the early observations, in which the planet had been mistaken for a star. And when the two orbits, as deduced from these two sets of observations, were compared together, it might have been expected that the tracks they indicated for the moving body would be identical. But this anticipation was not realised. The orbit of Uranus as indicated by later observations was not the same as that indicated by the earlier observations.

This disagreement excited much interest among astronomers. Bouvard published in 1821 an account of the movement of Uranus in which he dwelt upon the discrepancies, and he shewed that they could only be accounted for by supposing that they were due to some extraneous and unknown influence which disturbed the movements of the planet. Of course the known planets, Jupiter and Saturn, exercised their disturbing effect upon Uranus also, but these could be allowed for, and when this was done it was found that there were discrepancies still outstanding. He even went so far as to suggest that this extraneous influence was perhaps due to the attraction of some unknown planet which circulated in an orbit exterior to that of Uranus.

A magnificent mathematical problem was thus suggested. It was no less than the investigation of the orbit of this unknown planet from the effect which its attraction produced on the movements of Uranus.

§ 154. **The Discovery of Neptune.** If there were indeed an outer planet, certain facts with reference to it might at all events be predicted from the analogy of the planets already known. It might fairly be assumed that this outer planet revolved around the Sun in a nearly circular orbit, and that the plane in which it moved was practically coincident with the plane in which all the other great planets revolved. It was also possible to take a still further step by a reasonable conjecture as to what the distance of the new planet from the Sun might be expected to be. There exists indeed a very curious relation which connects together, in an approximate fashion, the distances of the important planets. This relation is generally known by the name of Bode's Law. We must be careful to distinguish it from such laws as those of Kepler, the latter are founded on the laws of gravitation, and thus rest on a mathematical basis, while Bode's Law must be described, at least so far as our present knowledge extends, as purely empirical. It appears to be true, but mathematicians have not yet been able to assign any reason why it should be so. In any case we have to note that its truth is only of an approximate character.

It is however worthy of enunciation. We write the following series of numbers

$$0, \ 3, \ 6, \ 12, \ 24, \ 48, \ 96.$$

It is easy to remember this series by the circumstance that after the two first figures have been written down each number is double the one which precedes it. Let us now alter this series by adding four to each of these numbers, the row of figures then becomes

$$4, \ 7, \ 10, \ 16, \ 28, \ 52, \ 100.$$

This series of figures bears a remarkable relation to the Solar System. With the exception of the fifth figure, 28, the numbers we have set down are approximately proportional to the distances of the several principal planets from the Sun. We may regard the number 28 as representing collectively the positions of the asteroids. In fact, if we denote the distance of the Earth from the Sun by the number 10, we may represent the distances of the various bodies of the Solar System as follows :

Mercury	Venus	Earth	Mars	Asteroids	Jupiter	Saturn
3·9	7·2	10	15·2	28	52·9	95·4

These numbers agree moderately well with those indicated by Bode's law. It was further found when Uranus was discovered that its distance from the Sun, as represented by the law, would be 196, which does not differ much from 191·8, which is found by multiplying the actual distance of Uranus, expressed in terms of the mean radius of the Earth's orbit, by 10. Thus the law of Bode gave a sort of suggestion as to what the distance of the planet should be if there were such a planet revolving beyond Uranus. On the same scale as those already adopted the law would indicate 388 as the distance of the planet immediately outside Uranus, and this served in some degree as a guide to the unknown body. It should however be mentioned that as the results actually turned out the law of Bode was in this case considerably astray. The actual distance of Neptune was discovered to be no more than 300·4.

The search for this unknown object was undertaken independently by two mathematicians, by Le Verrier in France and by Adams in England. It was shewn by Le Verrier that these discrepancies could be completely reconciled by the existence of an outer planet, of which he determined the orbit. He was indeed enabled to predict the place of the planet so accurately that on the memorable night of September 23, 1846, this new planet was actually discovered by Dr Galle, at Berlin, on making a search in the very spot to which the indications of Le Verrier guided him. A search had however been commenced previously by Professor Challis at Cambridge in accordance with the calculations of Adams, and Challis had actually observed the planet with the Northumberland Equatorial on August the 4th, and 12th, 1846. There can be little doubt that from Challis's observations, whenever they came to be discussed, the planetary nature of the object would have been fully recognised. Unfortunately this discussion was not undertaken until after Dr Galle's observations had been announced, and so the actual priority of the discovery was lost to Adams. The scientific world has long since agreed that the credit for this brilliant discovery must be equally shared between Le Verrier and Adams.

The planet Neptune brought to light in this astonishing manner is not visible to the unaided eye. It will, generally speaking, be ranked as a star of the 8th magnitude. Under a high magnifying power the dimensions of the planet become more considerable and its circular disc can be perceived. The actual diameter of Neptune is about four times the diameter of the Earth. It is accompanied by a single satellite. This planet is, so far as we know, the outermost planet of the solar system. Nor is there any reason for thinking that there are any planets beyond it.

CHAPTER XII.

COMETS.

§ 155. Appearance of Comets. Besides the planets
and their satellites there are other bodies of a very different
character which belong also to the Solar System. These
bodies are Comets and Shooting Stars. A comet possesses
generally a nucleus of more or less brilliance, surrounded
with a vast quantity of nebulous material, which is often
extended in one direction so as to form a tail. Very
frequently, however, comets are not provided with this
appendage, and sometimes also the nucleus is very faint,
or is entirely wanting. Comets vary greatly as to brightness ; in the majority of cases these objects are merely
telescopic, but sometimes they are brilliant and most
striking phenomena. For instance, the comet of 1680 is
said to have had a tail so great that it stretched across
the sky through an arc equal to 90°, and others have been
recorded with tails even still greater.

A comet is generally visible for only a brief period.
It will first appear suddenly in some region where there
has been nothing previously to attract attention, and then
from day to day it increases in brightness and varies in
shape ; sometimes it remains visible for a few weeks,
sometimes for months ; occasionally it passes so close to
the Sun that it becomes invisible for a while, and then
again it will be restored to view on passing to the other side

of the Sun, and gradually receding it becomes smaller and ultimately disappears.

§ 156. **Movement of Comets.** We owe the explanation of the movements of the comets to Newton. He saw that, as a consequence of the law of gravitation, each object submitted to the attraction of the Sun must revolve in a conic section around the Sun. The conic sections in which the several planets move are ellipses, and in like manner many of the comets revolve also in ellipses. But the shape of the ellipse is, generally speaking, very different in the two cases. All the important planets have elliptic orbits which differ but little from the circular form. They do not move in orbits which are highly eccentric, but orbits of this kind are found to prevail amongst the comets. The elliptic tracks in which comets revolve are generally of a high degree of eccentricity.

Newton's principle however shewed that any conic section was a possible form of orbit under the influence of a centre of attractive force such as that exerted by the Sun. Now there are three forms of conic sections, the ellipse, the parabola, and the hyperbola. By the movements of the planets we were provided with excellent illustrations of revolution in elliptic orbits; the comets give us illustrations of movements in the two other types of curve. The great majority of comets move in what is known as the parabola. There is a fundamental difference between movement in an ellipse and movement in a parabola, inasmuch as the ellipse is a closed curve, while the parabola is not. It therefore follows that if a comet be moving in an elliptic track it will return to its original position after the lapse of a number of years, greater or less, according as the dimensions of that track are greater or less. In such a case the comet will be periodic. We may expect it to appear over and over again, and some very striking comets are of this character.

The most famous example of this class is the comet of Halley, which revolves in about seventy-five years. It was last seen in 1835 and will be therefore due again about 1910. The movement of a body along a parabolic track is of a very different character. The comet will advance towards the Sun, it will sweep round the Sun and then it will commence to retreat. As, however, the parabola is not a closed curve, it follows that the object thus started will never again return. Most of the famous comets, of which the history is recorded, appear to have been of this parabolic class, they make one, and only one, apparition. The most notable comet in the memory of those still living appeared in 1858, during the Autumn of which year it attracted universal attention. This was a comet of the kind to which I have referred, which have only a single recorded appearance.

§ 157. **Photographs of Comets.** The photographic processes which are now so useful in astronomy have been of special advantage in the endeavour to represent the comets. As there is no phenomenon ever witnessed in the heavens more striking than a great comet, so there is certainly none which is apparently more suited for that particular kind of study which the camera permits. The growth of the photographic art has been, however, so recent that up to the present no comet which could be described as really splendid has presented itself for examination by our plates. Astronomers are still anxiously awaiting the display of another cometary spectacle similar to that which burst forth in 1858.

§ 158. **Swift's Comet, 1892.** Some of the most remarkable portraits of comets which have yet been obtained are due to Professor Barnard when he was at the Lick Observatory. We shew here a picture of Swift's Comet taken by Barnard in the year 1892. It may be regarded as exhibiting the structure typical of such

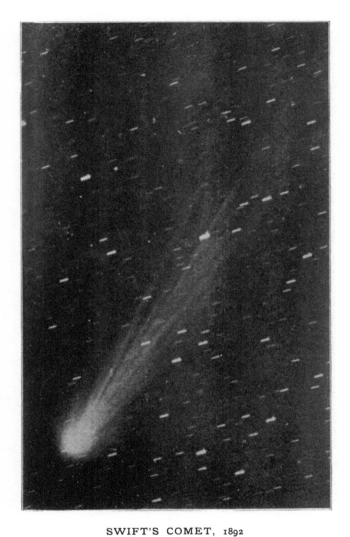

SWIFT'S COMET, 1892

Photographed by PROF. BARNARD, April 19, 1892

To face page 148

bodies generally. There is first of all the more or less circular head, and then there is the tail which extends to a very great distance. Whatever may be thought of the dimensions which the tail appears to display as shewn on the plate, there can be no doubt that the actual length of this important feature extended to many millions of miles. It had long been known that the greater part of a comet is composed of materials of the flimsiest description. There appears to be nothing that is actually solid in any part of the body's mighty extent, and the tail consists of material which is specially rarefied and diffused. This is abundantly illustrated by the circumstance that very faint stars can be seen right through the thickness of the tail of the comet. In looking at such stars the line of vision actually pierces through a volume of cometary material hundreds of thousands of miles in thickness. Judging from its effects on the star, the comet's tail does not seem to possess as much opaque material as is in a light cloud floating on a summer sky. Faint stars would be completely extinguished by such a cloud, and yet we often see stars notwithstanding the interposition of a stupendous thickness of comet. This fact sufficiently demonstrates the extraordinary rarity of the materials of which a comet is composed.

An interesting feature connected with the comet is brought out very strikingly by the photograph. For such pictures long exposures are indispensable. The objects are sometimes so delicate that a detailed picture cannot be obtained in less than an hour. But we must remember that in the course of an hour the apparent diurnal motion of the heavens carries both the stars and the comets through a considerable distance. If therefore the telescope were kept fixed during the time of exposure intelligible pictures of the celestial bodies would be impossible. It is accordingly necessary to guide the telescope so that we shall follow the comet in such a way as to enable the image of the body always to be impressed on the same part of the plate.

This is a delicate operation, and it requires much care on the part of the astronomer, who is directing the instrument, while the exposure is in progress. But in this particular application of celestial photography a very interesting point must be observed. The comet is all the time pursuing its own orbit and consequently, while the exposure has lasted, the comet experiences a displacement relative to the surrounding stars. As, however, it is the comet which it is desired to represent the telescope has been always directed to that object. It follows that the images of the stars which would of course have been sharply marked points if the telescope had been guided by their movements, were transformed into little streaks. These streaks may be regarded as exhibiting both in direction and in magnitude the distance through which the comet had moved during the time of the exposure.

§ 159. Direction of Comet's Tails. A further instructive point is brought out by this picture. It will be noted that the tail of the comet does not appear to stream out along the direction which is defined by the star streak. The tail of the comet does not lie along its track in the same way as the sparks from a sky-rocket lie along the track which the sky-rocket has pursued. The tail of the comet has assumed a position which is imposed by the direction in which the Sun lies relatively to it. Indeed, it is a general rule that the tail of a comet points away from the Sun, and that it does so independently of the direction in which the comet may at the time happen to be moving.

§ 160. Discovery of Comets by Photography. The camera has also been the means of discovering at least one comet which had not been previously detected by the ordinary method followed in searching for such objects. Professor Barnard when taking a photograph of the stars in the ordinary way was as usual guiding the telescope by a star on the picture. When the plate was developed the stars appeared to be points of light, as of course they should. There was however one object on the plate which did not present the appearance of a point, it rather appeared as an ill-defined streak. This was clearly an indication of something which had moved relatively to the stars during the time of the exposure. A little further examination shewed that this was indeed a new comet, whose existence was thus betrayed by the fact of its displacement.

Yet one more achievement of the camera in the study of the comets may be mentioned. It has opened up a field of possible developments in the future. It has been frequently found that the photographic plate will represent objects which cannot be seen by the human eye. A comet appeared with the tail about 2° in length so far as mere telescopic examination would display it. It is however certain that the tail of this comet was a very much larger structure than the mere telescopic picture would lead us to suppose, for the photographs display a tail not less than five times as long.

CHAPTER XIII.

§ 161. How a Shooting Star becomes visible. An ordinary shooting star is really a very small object. Probably the shooting stars in a shower are bodies comparable in size with the pebbles on a gravel walk. The shooting star is rendered visible to us only by the illumination generated by the heat attending its plunge into the atmosphere with which the Earth is surrounded. In open space the little object which is to be presently transformed into a streak of splendour is rushing along with a speed one hundred times as great as that with which the swiftest rifle bullet is animated, for in the emptiness of space there is no resistance to motion. Directly the missile finds itself in contact with the atmosphere it experiences tremendous obstruction. As it rushes through the air it becomes warmed by friction; the friction is indeed so great that the object becomes red hot and white hot, until at last it is actually melted and transformed into a streak of brilliant vapour. Thus it is that we see what is called a shooting star.

On almost any night that is clear the careful observer will see several such objects. The majority of these are such exceedingly small bodies as to be dissipated during their flight through the atmosphere. But from time to time some of larger size are observed, and in some cases even they have partially survived the fiery ordeal which the atmospheric resistance presents and a portion of their solid mass has fallen on the surface of the Earth. These objects are then called meteorites.

§ 162. **Showers of Shooting Stars.** It occasionally happens that shooting stars appear in vast multitudes, forming what is known as a shooting star shower. The meteors of a shooting star shower are found in each case to diverge or radiate from a particular point, or from a small area of the sky, and in general the appearance of each shower is confined to a particular time of year. Thus there are the shooting stars, to mention only the most important, radiating from a point in the constellation Perseus which are, from this circumstance, called Perseids. These are met with every year in the second week of August. There are also the Andromedids, whose radiant point is situated in the constellation Andromeda and which are only seen about November 27. But the most interesting of all the periodical shooting star showers are the Leonids, whose radiant point is in the constellation Leo and which are met with about the middle of November. There are some disturbing causes, which we need not at present consider, tending to bring about the reappearance of this shower at a later and later date at each recurrence, but at present it is to be looked out for between November 14th and 16th. Those who were fortunate enough to have witnessed the superb display of shooting stars on the 13th November, 1866, will probably agree that it was the most impressive spectacle they ever beheld in the heavens.

§ 163. **The periodicity of the Leonids.** The recurrence of this shooting star shower is remarkable. They make a special appearance on an average every thirty-three years and a quarter. It may well be asked how we can venture to predict a shooting star shower with any reasonable expectation of success. It may at once be admitted that we cannot attempt to foretell the occurrence of shooting star showers with the same feeling of absolute certainty as we have in the prediction of an eclipse of the Sun or the Moon. The latter depend only on the relative positions of the Sun, the Moon, and the Earth, and thus involve only considerations which are in all respects known to us. In the case of the movements of the shooting stars the conditions are by no means so definite as they are in the case of an eclipse.

Each year when the critical date in November comes round, astronomers are accustomed to expect rather more shooting stars than are generally to be seen on other nights of the year. But the display of these Leonids has by no means the same significance every year. Sometimes a November will pass in which but few meteors will be noticed specially belonging to this group, and in most other years the Leonids observed by astronomers do not form any spectacle sufficient to command the particular attention of the public. But it has sometimes happened that the arrival of the middle of November has been marked by a display of countless thousands of shooting stars, exhibiting a spectacle only to be described as sublime.

§ 164. **Former Showers.** For nearly a thousand years such phenomena have from time to time been noticed. Early chroniclers, who had not the faintest idea of the true character of the apparition which to their astonishment suddenly burst forth, set down accounts of what they saw. No doubt these accounts of celestial portents have but little pretension to scientific accuracy, but they give us at least the dates which are all important for our purpose. From a comparison of various observations it thus became manifest that the great displays occurred at intervals of about thirty-three years. We cannot indeed affirm that splendid showers of November meteors have actually been observed at every successive interval of thirty-three years, the records that have been preserved, or at all events the records that have been discovered, are not sufficiently complete to enable this to be affirmed. It must be remembered that if the night happened to be overcast—and this, in most northern climates, is a circumstance by no means unlikely in the middle of November—then the shooting stars would not be seen. It must also be remembered that as such displays could never be predicted by the early astronomers, who were totally ignorant of their real character, no organised arrangement could ever have been made for their observation, and consequently the accounts of such displays which have been preserved must be regarded merely as fortunate accidents. It may indeed have happened that great showers have taken place and have been observed, but that no records of such events have as yet been brought to light. It is even conceivable that records of great shooting star showers may still exist which have hitherto escaped those who have devoted special attention to the subject. We must therefore not be surprised if there are many gaps in the history of these Leonids. Since the year 902 A.D., when the earliest of these showers, so far at least as we know at present, was observed, there may have been thirty of these exceptional displays. Of these about a dozen are known historically ; as to the rest, testimony is silent.

But as might be expected we have had pretty full information on the subject so far as the present century is concerned. There was a great display of this particular shower in 1799 and there was another great display in 1833. Thus astronomers were led to the expectation that there would be a recurrence of this phenomena in 1866. I have already mentioned how wonderfully this prediction was fulfilled. It is the application of the same reasoning which leads us to the expectation that there will be a renewal of the great display of shooting stars at like intervals in the future.

§ 165. **Explanation of Periodic Showers.** Since the great display in 1866 we have learned much about the actual nature of these little objects and their movements, and we can now explain the causes of their appearance in great showers. I shall here set forth an outline of what is known of this periodical shower.

The Leonids which we see in November belong to a mighty shoal containing unnumbered myriads of little objects. This vast host sweeps along a great celestial highway which forms an oval figure nearly two thousand million miles long, each, as a minute planet, obeying the attraction of the Sun. Pursuing this vast track the shoal of meteors make their circuit round the Sun. Notwithstanding the high speed with which these objects move, the course that they have to get round is so vast that not less than $33\frac{1}{4}$ years are required by them to accomplish one complete journey. The path in which our Earth makes its annual circuit, crosses the track of the shooting stars. In general the main shoal of little objects, although spread for many millions of miles along the track, does not happen to be at the point of crossing when the Earth reaches the same point, and so we encounter only the few stragglers which may happen to lie along the great highway. These provide for us the Leonids generally encountered in the middle of each November.

Once every thirty-three years, however, the principal part of the shoal of these little bodies arrives at the point of crossing just at the same time as the Earth. The Earth may then plough its way through the uncounted myriads and the result is a grand display of Leonids.

CHAPTER XIV.

§ 166. The Number of the Stars. Every new telescopic discovery tends to give us larger ideas as to the scale on which the universe is built. Our unaided eyes can detect at one view perhaps two thousand stars of varied degrees of magnitude strewn over the heavens. When we use a telescope to help us, even though that telescope may be of but very moderate power, the number of stars is increased ten- or twenty-fold. With larger instruments the stars are increased a hundred-fold, a thousand-fold, even ten thousand-fold or more. If discarding our visual observation we employ the photographic plate, bewildering millions of stars are displayed of whose existence we were previously unaware. The number of stars in such a picture may be conjectured from the photograph of the clusters in Perseus referred to in § 170.

§ 167. Proper Motion. Many of the stars possess what is called *proper motion.* If the place of a star on the heavens be carefully determined at one epoch and if the place of the same star be again determined years afterwards, when allowance has been made for the apparent displacement arising from precession, aberration and nutation, which affect every star according to its position in the heavens, it will not unfrequently appear that the position of the star has shifted in the intervening period. Such observations are of much delicacy, for the movements which the stars make seem to us very small on account of their distances, even though such movements may be intrinsically gigantic. A star might be moving faster than the Earth moves, or faster indeed than any planet of our system, and yet in the course of a couple of centuries the actual distance which such a star would seem to have travelled on the surface of the heavens would not be greater than the apparent diameter of the Moon. If the star were free from all disturbing effects, such movements would proceed uniformly, but if the star were acted upon by the attraction of some other body its movement would be correspondingly deranged. In this way it will sometimes happen that the movements of the star will be appreciably affected by the attraction of another body in its vicinity. It is not the least necessary that the attracting body should be luminous; all that is required is that it be massive enough and near enough to the star to produce a considerable effect. In the movements of some of the stars we discover unmistakable indications that they are influenced by the attraction of other bodies in their neighbourhood. In fact, the more closely we scrutinise the proper motion of different stars the more do we perceive the irregularities with which such movements are affected.

§ 168. **Invisible Stars.** The interest of such observations is very great. From the influence which such objects exert on the movements of stars that happen to be visible we learn the existence of massive celestial bodies which we have never seen and can never hope to see. Indeed everything we know about the stars teaches us that the quantity of matter which the Universe contains, even without going beyond the telescopic distances, is probably

CLUSTER (M. 13) HERCULIS

W. E. WILSON

To face page 159

hundreds of times, or thousands of times, and it may be millions of times, greater than the total mass of the stars which are visible to us.

§ 169. **Star Clusters.** There is no spectacle more astounding to a student of the heavens than that of a great star-cluster. It is well known that in this respect those astronomers whose lot is cast in the Southern hemisphere are more favoured than are those who live in Europe or North America. The most glorious star-cluster that the firmament contains is that in the constellation Centaur.

It sometimes happens that when an astronomer turns his attention towards a so-called cluster of stars he will think that the cluster ought to be described as a part of the sky where the stars are a little richer, a little more abundantly distributed, than usual, rather than as a distinct object evidently indicating a number of stars associated together in a separate system. But no such feeling is possible when we examine such a wonderful object as the great cluster of the Centaur. Sir John Herschel studied it and made a beautiful drawing of its details on the occasion of his memorable observation at the Cape of Good Hope. It has ever since attracted the attention of every astronomer who has been so fortunate as to be able to point the telescope in its direction.

§ 170. **Great Clusters in Hercules and Perseus.** In our Northern hemisphere the most remarkable of these globular clusters is that in the constellation of Hercules. This beautiful celestial object has been here represented in a reproduction of a photograph taken by Mr W. E. Wilson at his own Observatory in Westmeath. There is also a superb object of the kind in the sword handle of Perseus. In this case there are two groups of stars close together, and when a powerful telescope is employed the multitude of these stars and their intrinsic lustre combine to form a most wonderful spectacle. This object and the region of the Milky Way surrounding it is here shewn. The photograph from which this picture of celestial scenery is reproduced was taken by Prof. E. E. Barnard at the Lick Observatory, California.

§ 171. **The Pleiades.** A very well-known star-cluster is the famous group known as the Pleiades. From the very earliest times this beautiful asterism arrested attention. It was clearly not the result of chance that a number of conspicuous stars should be so closely associated. It can easily be shewn that if all the stars in heaven had been scattered quite at random over the skies, the probabilities would have been very many millions to one against the occurrence of a collection of stars like the Pleiades in the positions where we actually find them. It is hence impossible to refuse to accept the belief that the stars in the Pleiades must belong to some organised system. They are undoubtedly a group of associated bodies owning probably a common origin and with many common features in their structure.

The interest with which this famous constellation was always regarded became greatly increased when by the extension of our knowledge we began to learn something of the sizes and weights of the different bodies of which it is composed. So long as the stars were thought to be merely little objects not possessing any great intrinsic brightness, there was no reason to regard the Pleiades with greater interest than belongs to a collection of celestial gems arranged with exquisite beauty of detail. But when it was realised that the group in question was in truth a collection of globes sunlike in dimensions and lustre, the true importance of the Pleiades became recognised.

The individual stars forming this cluster have long engaged the attention of astronomers. First and most brilliant among them is that known as Alcyone, it is a star

MILKY WAY NEAR CLUSTER IN PERSEUS

Photographed by PROF. BARNARD, NOV. 3, 1893

To face page 160

of the third magnitude. Besides Alcyone there are five other important stars in the constellation. The brightest of these are known as Electra and Atlas, each of which is of about the fourth magnitude. In the descending scale of lustre we have Maia, near the fifth, Merope and Taygeta are much about the same. The seventh star of the Pleiades is Celaeno ; it is only occasionally to be seen with the unaided eye. Acute vision will, however, shew many other stars in this famous group. Some observers gifted with exceptional vision have been able to see twelve of the Pleiades. No doubt there are quite this number of stars in the group bright enough to be visible to most ordinary eyes, if they were presented as isolated spots on the dark sky, but the fact that the Pleiades is so crowded increases the difficulty of discriminating the fainter points.

With the slightest telescopic power the number of visible Pleiades is seen to be enormously increased. No less than sixty-nine stars can be seen with a very small instrument which can easily be held in the hand. But it must not be supposed that the number of stars just referred to includes all those in the group. Their number is indeed vastly greater. With every increase in the power of the telescope more and more stars are brought within the range of vision. And what the most powerful telescope is able to render visible to the eye is vastly transcended by the results obtained by taking a photograph of long exposure. The brothers Henri, in Paris, have obtained more than two thousand star-images on a single plate directed to the Pleiades. Nor is there the least reason to think that the full tale of stars in the group has been even yet ascertained. Each increase in the sensibility of the plate or in the duration of its exposure invariably brings with it an increased number of the stars which are represented.

We shall explain in § 185 how the distances of the

stars are determined. It will however frequently happen
that the stars are so remote that the method becomes
inapplicable. All we can then do is to determine a certain
minimum distance which we can say is certainly exceeded.
And in this case all we know about the distance of the
Pleiades amounts to the statement that this group must be
millions of times as remote from our Earth as is the Sun.
This leads to a very interesting conclusion. We can
estimate what the brightness of our Sun would be if it
were transferred to a distance such as that which we know
must be at least the distance of the Pleiades. It seems
perfectly certain that under such circumstances the Sun
would send us less light than the very faintest Pleiad
which the keenest eye can detect. We do not indeed
assert that the Sun is larger than every one of the two
thousand and upward stars of which the Pleiades is composed. It is however certain that Alcyone and probably
some of the other brilliant gems of the constellation must
be hundreds of times more lustrous than our own orb of
day. A planet revolving around Alcyone in an orbit as
great as that which Neptune, the outermost of our planets,
describes around the Sun, would only circulate through
a wholly insignificant portion of the mighty cluster; so
close indeed would it appear to Alcyone that, even if it
were a bright object like Alcyone itself, a good telescope
would be required to see the two objects apart.

§ 172. **Spectra of the Stars in the Pleiades.**
Modern spectroscopic research has brought evidence of a
very striking character to shew the common origin and the
common physical character of the stars in the Pleiades.
It is known of course that the light in the spectrum of a
star is eminently characteristic of that star. Indeed it is
doubtful if any two stars in the heavens would manifest
exactly the same spectrum if we were able to see all the
lines that the spectrum of each contained. Professor

DUMB-BELL NEBULA

W. E. WILSON

Pickering, who has devoted himself with such skill to the study of the spectra of the stars, has examined the light which is emitted to us from the principal stars of the Pleiades. It has been found that their spectra are substantially of one type. This is a confirmation of the statement that the stars in the Pleiades form an associated group.

§ **173. Nebulae.** There are a number of objects in the heavens which are termed nebulae. One or two of these are visible to the unaided eye, but the rest, to the number of some seven thousand or more, require telescopic power and often telescopes of very high power indeed. Many of these objects are strictly gaseous in their character. By the method of spectrum analysis it has been shewn that they contain hydrogen as well as, in all probability, certain other substances.

One of the most remarkable of these objects is well known to every astronomical observer. This is the Great Nebula in the Swordhandle of Orion which seems to be a huge chaotic mass of glowing gas. Although this object has been under observation for 200 years and whole books have been written on the phenomena it presents, yet we are still a very long way indeed from a complete knowledge of the conditions under which it exists.

We here reproduce a remarkable photograph taken by Mr W. E. Wilson. This is the "Dumb-bell" in Vulpecula. In it we see an approach to a symmetrical form, the mass being bounded at its northern and southern limits by approximately circular arcs of increased brightness.

In the constellation of Andromeda a faint patch of indistinct brightness can just be detected with the naked eye on a clear night. This is the Great Nebula in Andromeda and is the only true nebula which was known before the days of the telescope. This has always been one of the most interesting telescopic objects of its class in the

11—2

heavens, but certain features were never properly understood until the photographic plate was applied by Dr Isaac
Roberts to supplement the powers of the human eye.

Then it was seen that it consisted of an enormous mass
of glowing material surrounded by separate rings of a
similar, but less intensely, bright appearance. We seem
to be looking down obliquely on the plane in which the
rings are arranged so that they appear to be projected into
somewhat elongated ellipses. A photograph of this nebula
shewing also Holmes' Comet was taken by Prof. Barnard
on Nov. 10, 1892, and is here reproduced.

Astronomers have not yet succeeded in determining
how far from the Earth this wonderful object must be, and
consequently it is impossible to say with any pretence to
precision what its dimensions can be. But we may set a
lower limit beyond which it must lie, since otherwise it
would have afforded evidence of an annual displacement
which would have enabled us to measure its distance. We
may thus with confidence say that the great nebula in
Andromeda is at least 100,000 times the Sun's distance
from us. From the apparent size of the object as seen in
the sky we know that its exterior diameter cannot be less
than $\frac{1}{25}$th part of its distance. Hence it follows that this
nebula must measure *at least* 400,000 millions of miles from
side to side, or more than 70 times the diameter of the orbit
of Neptune. This is the very lowest estimate, and we should
probably not be erring on the side of excess if we stated
that the true dimensions are quite ten times as much as
the figures given.

One of the most interesting discoveries recently made,
in connexion with nebulae, has revealed to us that some of
these objects, including indeed the very greatest nebulae,
are totally invisible. They are not to be seen by the
eye even with the help of the best telescopes, and can
only be discerned by the photographic plate. A remarkable

THE GREAT NEBULA IN ANDROMEDA AND
HOLMES' COMET

Photographed by Prof. Barnard, Nov. 10, 1892

To face page 164

instance of a nebula of this kind is presented in connexion
with the group of stars in the Pleiades. When a photograph is taken with an exposure of not less than an hour, a
nebula with considerable luminous density and of enormous
volume is seen to cover the whole group of stars. The
nebula is, however, of very variable brightness in different
parts of the cluster. When such a plate as this was first
taken it was hard to read aright the tale that it unfolded.
It might at first be natural to attribute the phenomena
revealed on the plate to some blemishes in the process of
development, or to some accidental disorder in the plate
itself. But when one photograph after another displayed
precisely the same luminous configuration, when telescopes
of very varying sizes invariably reproduced the nebula
with the same general characteristics, when the nebula was
alike apparent on photographs obtained by telescopes which
refracted, and by telescopes which reflected, then it became
manifest that the observed phenomena could not be explained away as arising from any accidents in the operation
or from any defects in the plate.

The lesson that we thus learn with regard to the
Pleiades is very instructive. If the evidence had seemed
insufficient to convince us hitherto that these stars really
constituted a group bound together by physical bonds, the
facts now brought forward would have dispelled such a
notion. The nebula includes within its mighty compass
the stars of the Pleiades. It would be difficult to
suppose that this nebula was an isolated volume of vapour
which happened by some chance to be located directly on
the line connecting the Solar System and the Pleiades. It
would not be reasonable to suppose that the great fire-
cloud had been casually projected on a remarkable group
of stars in the background. It would be just as unreason-
able to suppose that the group of stars has been casually
projected on the great nebula stretched as a curtain behind

it. We cannot withhold our assent from the belief that the nebula and the group of stars together form one majestic object in the firmament.

§ 174. Double Stars. It frequently happens that a star which to the unaided eye would appear as a single object is shewn in the telescope to consist of two stars close together. These objects are known as double stars, and their number is such that it is almost impossible to suppose that the contiguity in which they lie is always, or even frequently, accidental. Everyone who is accustomed to use a telescope is familiar with many of those double stars, which form indeed some of the most interesting telescopic spectacles that the heavens have to shew. Some of these are easy objects, that is to say, a very moderate degree of telescopic power will suffice to demonstrate the astonishing fact that the star, which to the unaided eye looks like an ordinary star consisting of a single globe, is in reality a pair of associated globes, so close together that the eye is not able to distinguish them separately until the magnifying power of the telescope has been called into requisition. In many cases these pairs of stars are so close together that a demand has to be made on the very highest powers which can be applied to the telescope in order to exhibit the two objects as separate points. Indeed it is well known that the criterion of the performance of a telescope is generally given by the capability which it shews for dividing the two components of a double star. We may give one illustration to shew the apparent proximity in which the two components of a double star will sometimes lie in the heavens. A good telescope, such as can now be found in all public observatories and in many private hands, will suffice to separate two nearly equal stars if the angular distance between them be one second. With the help of telescopes of the very highest class pairs of stars which lie much closer still can be separated.

Of course it will be understood that when we speak of the proximity of the two components of a double star we mean that they *appear* very close together on the sky and the distance by which the pair is separated from the terrestrial observer must be borne in mind. Even the closest pair which has ever been separated by the most powerful telescope must still have a distance of many million miles between its components. Indeed we know that if an observer on one of these stars could perceive the Earth, the distance between it and the Sun would appear to him, from the position in which he is placed, quite as small as do the apparent distances between the two components of many of the double stars appear to us.

We should, however, mention that many of the pairs of objects, which are usually spoken of as double stars, are not to be regarded as forming systems of the same character as those which we have been here describing and which are known as binary systems. It may of course happen that two stars which are in no way connected lie so nearly in line with the Earth, that when viewed from the Earth they appear close together in the sky, though as a matter of fact one of these stars may be ten times, or a hundred times, as far from us as the other. Objects of this class are not spoken of as a binary pair. Their proximity is merely casual, depending on the accident that the line joining them is directed towards the Earth. Such pairs of stars are of course not physically related, but it is often not easy to distinguish such pairs from genuine binaries. There is, however, one method sometimes available for discriminating between a pair of stars which are merely optically double, and a genuine binary pair. As we have mentioned already, many of the stars of all classes are animated by what are called proper movements. As each such star is borne along it drifts relatively to the other stars which happen to lie contiguous to its track. In the course of many years a star endowed with considerable proper motion may thus drift away from another star which seemed originally to lie close to it. If however the two members of a pair of stars were physically associated, then in the drift of one it would necessarily be accompanied by the other and the two would thus drift in company relatively to the other stars in the vicinity. In this way we are often provided with a criterion by which a binary star may be distinguished from a pair which is merely optically double.

§ 175. **Binary Stars.** In the case of a genuine binary pair, of which the stars not only seem to be, but are in fact, close together,—close that is to say as compared to the distance by which we are separated from them,—they revolve about each other in consequence of their mutual attraction. The movements are indeed conducted in conformity with Kepler's laws, and in the case of some of the more rapidly moving binaries it is extremely interesting to watch the way in which the relative positions of the two stars are observed to shift year after year. By making a series of measurements of their relative positions, we are frequently enabled to determine the track of one of these objects around the other, and to ascertain the number of years in which its revolution is accomplished. In some cases the period in which the stars revolve does not exceed six or seven years. In other cases, however, the periodic time mounts up to centuries.

§ 176. **Mass of a Binary.** One of the most interesting consequences that can be deduced from observations of the binary stars is the determination of the masses of the stars forming such a pair. If we know the dimensions of their orbits as well as the periodic times in which the revolutions are accomplished, we are able to tell the masses concerned in the attraction, just as we are able to find the mass of the planet from the revolution of its satellite. In order to obtain the actual size of the orbit we must know the distance of the pair from the Sun, and as this is known for only a very limited number of stars, this method is not at present of very wide application. Seeing that the stars are suns we naturally desire to utilize the information thus gained to make a comparison between the masses of the stars and the mass of our own Sun. The circumstances of a few binary stars permit us to determine their weights. Some of the binary stars are found to be about equal in weight to the Sun while others are by no means so heavy. Many are, however, far heavier than the great orb. We may in fact regard our Sun as a star of average magnitude, in so far at least as the information given to us by double stars is concerned.

§ 177. **Colours of Double Stars.** A beautiful feature connected with the double stars is found in the circumstance that the component orbs are frequently tinged with different hues. In many cases the tints of the two stars are beautifully contrasted, and sometimes the colours may be said to be complementary. Among the most famous of coloured pairs is the object known as Beta in the constellation of the Swan. One of its components possesses a beautiful topaz colour, while the other is of an emerald hue. Indeed in several cases the lesser of the two components of a double star displays a bluish or a violet tinge, and this is the more remarkable when it is observed that, unless in association with another star forming a binary pair, blue stars are almost unknown.

§ 178. **Triple Stars.** Much additional interest is often imparted by the circumstance that one of the two components will itself be found to be a double star. There is a famous pair of this class in Andromeda (Gamma Andromedae), the smaller component of which possesses an exquisite blue colour. By a very good telescope this component can be itself resolved into two little blue stars so close as to be incapable of being distinguished separately by any instrument which is not first-rate.

§ 179. **Multiple Stars.** In many cases there are several stars associated in one system, and the complexity of the movements in groups of this kind would baffle the skill of the most consummate mathematician. Up to the present, however, mathematicians have had but little opportunity for even attempting to investigate the mechanical subtleties of these elaborate stellar systems. Not until many more observations have been accumulated will it be possible to attempt any investigations of this kind with hopes of success.

§ 180. **Spectroscopic Binaries.** One of the most striking discoveries which has been made in connexion with double stars in recent years teaches us that there are multitudes of binary pairs whose components are so close together that there is not the slightest chance of our ever being able to see them separately, even if our telescopes were hundreds of times more powerful than those which are at present available. That certain stars, which all our telescopes would shew as single, must be double in reality has however been demonstrated from the fact that when the light received from them has been passed through the spectroscope to a photographic plate it gives unmistakable evidence of having emanated not from a single source but from two contiguous bodies in rapid motion relatively to each other. This is shewn by the fact that certain lines in the spectrum present themselves as double when one of the stars is approaching and the other is receding, while when both stars are moving across the line of vision the two lines coincide. In this manner it has been demonstrated that there are pairs of suns so close together that they revolve around each other in a few days, and from an examination of a sufficient series of such photographs it has been possible to learn the dimensions of the orbit in which these components move as well as their periodic times and thus to ascertain their weight. This branch of research is at present merely in its infancy, but it seems to indicate that numbers of objects which still appear to be merely single stars must ultimately disclose themselves as double.

CHAPTER XV.

§ 181. Aberration of Light. Besides the diurnal movement of the stars, there are other apparent movements which are of the utmost importance alike in the Theory of Astronomy and in the work of the Observatory.

One of the most important is that which was discovered in 1726 by the illustrious astronomer Bradley from his observations of the star γ Draconis. It followed from his study of that star, that it seemed to describe a small elliptic path on the surface of the heavens. The length of the axis of the ellipse was about forty seconds of arc, and the period required to complete a circuit was one year exactly. Further study shewed that other stars had similar movements. A star at, or near, the pole of the ecliptic moved in a circular track. As the position of the star was nearer to the ecliptic, the ellipse became more and more eccentric until in the case of a star actually in the ecliptic the movement of the star was no more than an oscillation to and fro in a straight line. In every case however the length of the major axis was the same, i.e. 40″. In every case the major axis was parallel to the ecliptic, and in every case the period is exactly one year.

These circumstances pointed out that an explanation of the apparent movements must be in some way connected with the annual motion of the Earth in its orbit.

By a happy stroke of genius Bradley saw what the explanation must be, and his discovery is referred to as that of the aberration of Light.

Light travels at a speed which is about 186,000 miles a second, i.e. about 10,000 times as fast as the progress of the Earth in its orbit. If the velocity of light had been infinitely greater than the velocity of the Earth, then the telescope pointed to the apparent place of the star would be pointed to the true place. As however the velocity of light is not infinitely greater but only 10,000 times greater than the velocity of the Earth in its track, the telescope directed to the star has to be directed to a neighbouring point between the true place of the star and the point on the celestial sphere towards which the Earth is at the moment urging its way. This apparent shift in the place of the star can be shewn to produce all the phenomena observed under the title of aberration.

§ 182. Precession of the Equinoxes. In connexion with the places of the stars we have to consider the phenomenon discussed in § 104 which is known as the precession of the equinoxes. We have seen how the right ascension of a star is to be measured by the angular distance between the great circle passing through the pole and that star, and the great circle passing through the pole and the equinox. Let us suppose that observations of this kind are repeated from year to year, and to take a particular case, I shall suppose that of the star Sirius. If the right ascension of Sirius be determined year after year it will be found that the right ascension increases at the rate of 2·65 seconds per annum. This increase is not quite uniform. But that is its average amount, and the increase is continually going on in the same direction. If we take a considerable period of time as an illustration, then we learn that in a hundred years the right ascension of Sirius is increased by 265 seconds, that is by over four minutes. Now this movement must be due to an alteration either in Sirius or in the equinox, for we have said that the right ascension is the angle which Sirius and the equinox subtend at the pole of the celestial sphere. It is however found by comparing Sirius with other stars that Sirius remains practically stationary with regard to them, and hence we are assured that the vernal equinox must be itself in motion amongst the stars. The tendency is always for the right ascension to increase, which shews that the vernal equinox is always receding a little, so as to make it ever tend to come earlier and earlier on the meridian. This is the phenomenon which we call the precession of the equinox. I have mentioned the star Sirius, but a like result would have been obtained by considering the movements of any other star. In short all the stars would agree in shewing that there was this continuous movement constantly bringing the equinox around amongst the stars from east to west.

The equinox is however defined to be the point in which the ecliptic and the equator intersect each other. If therefore the equinox is in motion this point of intersection of the ecliptic and the equator is in motion. It therefore follows necessarily that either the great circle which we call the equator, or the great circle which we call the ecliptic, or it may happen to be both those circles, is in movement. Let us consider which of these three suppositions is the case. So far as the ecliptic is concerned we are assured that it has not any motion which will avail us for explaining the phenomenon in question, for the distances of all the stars as measured from it are found to remain practically unchanged. The track of the Sun as laid down through the stars does not alter appreciably. We are therefore reduced to attributing the movements known as precession to a shift of the equator along the ecliptic.

§ 183. Change in the Obliquity. With regard to the movements of the equator it may alter either by simply rotating around on the ecliptic, constantly preserving the same angle of inclination thereto, or it would be possible for the equator to alter its obliquity to the ecliptic, or it would be possible for the equator to have movements of both kinds. But it is certainly demonstrated that the obliquity of the ecliptic does not much alter. The obliquity is determined by measuring the polar distance of the Sun at midsummer and subtracting that from ninety degrees, and it is found that the obliquity, though not absolutely constant, still varies very slightly. Its changes in a period of twenty years would not amount to a seven-thousandth part of its total value. We may therefore from our present point of view treat the obliquity of the ecliptic as a constant quantity. We are therefore led to the conclusion that the precession of the equinoxes must be due to the movements of the equator around the ecliptic. A further examination shews that the amount of the precession is 50·24 seconds of arc annually. This is the annual change in the position of the intersection of the equator with the ecliptic measured along the ecliptic. This movement is no doubt a slow one, for it is easy to shew that a period of very little less than twenty-six thousand years must elapse to enable the equinox while moving at this rate to make a complete circuit of the ecliptic.

§ 184. Precessional Movement of the Pole. We can appreciate more clearly the nature of this movement by thinking of the pole of the equator, that is, of the celestial pole of the heavens, rather than of the equator itself. Since the angle between two great circles is equal to the angle between their poles, it follows that the distance of the pole of the ecliptic from the pole of the equator is equal to the obliquity of the ecliptic. As the ecliptic is a fixed circle, so the pole of the ecliptic is a fixed point amongst the stars. And as the obliquity is constant it follows that the pole of the equator must be describing a small circle on the celestial sphere around the pole of the ecliptic as its centre. The radius of this circle, that is the obliquity of the ecliptic, is 23° 27′ 8″, and the pole completes its revolution around the circle in a period of about twenty-six thousand years.

Notwithstanding the slowness of this motion, it is yet capable of producing most striking effects on the arrangements of the constellations relatively to the pole, as may be seen from Fig. 23, which represents the path of the pole

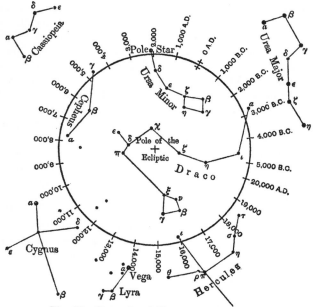

Fig. 23.　Precessional Movement of the Pole.

among the constellations. For instance, at present the star of the second magnitude which we call the Pole Star is within a degree and a quarter of the pole. But the nearness of the star and the pole is merely fortuitous. The pole is constantly moving on, and at present it so happens that the pole of the heavens is approaching the Pole Star. In a couple of centuries the Pole Star will in fact serve its purpose even still better than it does at present, because it will be within half a degree of the true pole. After this, however, the true pole will begin to separate from the Pole Star, and it may be mentioned that in about twelve thousand years the pole will have advanced to the opposite side of the circle which forms its orbit, and it will then have advanced to within about five degrees of the bright star Vega, which will accordingly serve as a Pole Star for many of the purposes for which our Pole Star is used at present.

§ 185. **Annual Parallax.** Connected with the annual movement of the Earth around the Sun is the phenomenon of annual parallax which is displayed by some of the stars. Seeing that the Sun's distance is about ninety-three millions of miles, it follows that an observer on the Earth who views a star on a particular day and again on this day six months does so from the opposite ends of a line which is a hundred and eighty-six millions of miles in length. So great a displacement in the position of the observer might be expected to carry with it a corresponding displacement in the apparent direction of the stars. If no great displacement can be perceived in the place of the star then all that can be said is that the distance of the star is so vast that the diameter of the Earth's orbit is merely an inconsiderable magnitude in reference thereto. This question has been studied very carefully and laboriously, because it provides us with the only possible means of solving the problem of the determination of the distances of the stars. We are to imagine a triangle whereof the vertex is a star and the base a diameter of the Earth's orbit. The observer when he is at one end of that diameter measures the angle between the Sun and the star. When he is at the other side of the orbit he measures again the angle between the Sun and the star. The length of the base being known and the two angles of the base being determined, then the solution of a triangle ought to give the position of the star. Such is in outline the method for determining the distance of a star. If, however, it so happened that the distance of the star was enormously great, then this triangle would be a very ill-conditioned one. The two sides of the triangle would be nearly parallel and the observed angles would be very nearly supplemental. Under such circumstances a minute error in observing the angles would entail an enormous difference in the concluded distance of the star. This is just the difficulty that arises. The stars one and all are so far off that even under the most favourable circumstances the two long sides of this triangle are each at least two hundred thousand times as long as the base. Nor does the difficulty end here. The direct measurement of the angles from the Sun to the star is attended with such practical difficulties that it would involve errors very much larger than the third angle of the triangle, and consequently this method would break down.

But by a modification of the process it has been found possible in several cases to determine the distances of stars. Let us suppose that we have two stars apparently close together, that is to say, lying within the same field of the telescope, but that in reality one of these stars is very much more distant than the other, suppose ten times as far. The change of the place of the observer from one end of the diameter of the Earth's orbit to the other will affect the places of both of these stars. But it will affect the nearer of the two stars, let us say, ten times as much as it will the more remote. In fact we may for the present consider that the remoter star has not moved at all and that the relative displacement has to be entirely attributed to the nearer of the two stars. The astronomer will therefore carefully measure the angle between the two stars which we have supposed to be visible in the same field of view in his telescope. This is one of the astronomical measurements which can be conducted with a very high degree of accuracy. We shall suppose that the measurements are repeated six months later, by which time the astronomer has been carried to the opposite diameter of the Earth.

In the adjoining figure (Fig. 24) the remoter star is supposed to be so far off that the lines, AS_2 and BS_2, drawn to it from two positions of the Earth at opposite sides of its orbit are indistinguishable from a pair of parallel lines. The nearer star, whose distance we want to measure, is represented at S_1. Then when the Earth is at A we measure the small angle S_1AS_2, and when at B, six months later, we measure the small angle S_1BS_2. Now since AS_2 and BS_2 are supposed to be sensibly parallel it follows that the angle $AOB = S_1BS_2$. But the angle

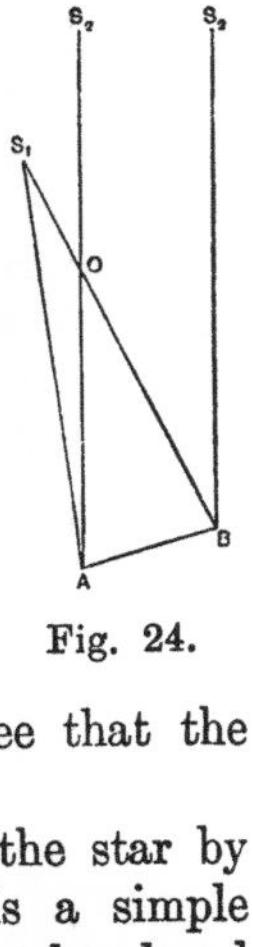

$$AS_1B = AOB - S_1AS_2,$$

Fig. 24.

wherefore $AS_1B = S_1BS_2 - S_1AS_2$. Thus we see that the angle AS_1B is determined.

But this angle is the angle subtended at the star by the diameter of the Earth's orbit, and it is a simple calculation to find out how far off the star must be placed in order that a line 186 millions of miles long should subtend an angle at it equal to that value which we find for AS_1B.

12—2

For example, if we found that on the 21st June $S_1AS_2 = 45''$, and on the 21st Dec. that $S_1BS_2 = 47''$, then of course $AS_1B = 2''$. But it can be easily shewn that in an isosceles triangle whose vertical angle is $2''$ the sides are 103,132 times as long as the base. Therefore the star in this case must be $103,132 \times 186,000,000$ miles, or more than 19 billions of miles away.

Half the angle AS_1B, or the angle subtended at the star by the radius of the Earth's orbit, is called the star's annual parallax.

Of course the triangle AS_1B will not generally be isosceles, as we have assumed for convenience of explanation, but calculation will enable the parallax to be found in other cases.

It may be remarked that no star has been found to have a parallax as large as $1''$, as we have supposed, from which we conclude that no star exists within a distance of 19 billions of miles of the Sun. The nearest star yet found is situated at a distance of 25 billions of miles.

The great majority of the objects which we see each night are at distances so great that they have not been determined. In most cases indeed there is little hope of determining them. This consideration gives us an impressive notion of the scale of the Sidereal System.

CHAPTER XVI.

CELESTIAL OBJECTS.

§ 186. The Northern and Southern Maps. To aid the beginner in identifying the different constellations and finding the names of important stars we give two maps on which many of the leading celestial objects are represented. These maps are called respectively the Northern Heavens and the Southern Heavens.

It is convenient for our present purpose to divide the surface of the celestial sphere into twenty parts here termed Regions.

A circle described round the North celestial pole as centre and with a radius of 25° includes every star of which the North Declination exceeds 65°. The area of this circle constitutes Region 1 as shown on the Northern map.

The zone of the celestial sphere from 65° to 20° of North Declination is divided into six equal Regions as shown in the Northern map. These Regions are severally designated by the numbers 2, 3, 4, 5, 6, 7.

The equatorial zone of the celestial sphere lying between 20° of North Declination and 20° of South Declination is divided into six equal Regions severally designated by the numbers 8, 9, 10, 11, 12, 13. These Regions are shown both on the Northern map and the Southern map but with a difference in their presentation.

The zone of the celestial sphere from 20° to 65° of South Declination is divided into six equal Regions as shown in the Southern map and these Regions are severally designated by the numbers 14, 15, 16, 17, 18, 19.

Finally a circle described round the South celestial Pole as centre and with a radius of 25° includes every star of which the South Declination exceeds 65°. The area of this circle constitutes Region 20 as shown on the Southern map.

Thus Regions 1—13 are in the Northern map and Regions 8—20 in the Southern map, the six equatorial Regions 8—13 being common to the two maps.

It will be noted that each equatorial region is inverted on either map when compared with the same Region as shown on the other map. To explain this we shall give an illustration from Region 9, which contains the constellation Orion.

An observer in Great Britain or Canada sees Orion due south at 10 p.m. local mean time in January. He notes Betelgeuze on the *upper* side of Orion and Rigel on the *lower* side while Sirius is to the East which is then on the left of the observer. Thus the heavens are represented in the Northern map.

If we imagine the observer to be travelling southwards with the quickness of thought he will find Orion climbing higher and higher in the heavens. When the observer has reached the Equator the Belt of Orion will be in his zenith. Pressing onwards and still facing south the observer enters the Southern Hemisphere and as he advances Orion will be descending towards the north part of the horizon. Let us suppose he has reached the south temperate regions and now desires to see Orion ; it is behind his back. He turns round to face the North. There is Orion, but its position appears inverted.

It is plain that the observer must find that the star

Northern Regions

Region		R.A.		Decl.		
1	The Pole Star ...			$+65°$ to $+90°$		
2	Cassiopeia	...	XXII to	II	$+20°$ „	$+65°$
3	Capella ...	...	II „	VI	„	„ „
4	Gemini ...	...	VI „	X	„	„ „
5	Ursa Major	...	X „	XIV	„	„ „
6	Hercules	...	XIV „ XVIII		„	„ „
7	Vega ...	...	XVIII „ XXII		„	„ „

Equatorial Regions

8	Cetus ...	...	0 to	IV	$-20°$ to $+20°$		
9	Sirius ...	...	IV „	VIII	„	„	„
10	Regulus...	...	VIII „	XII	„	„	„
11	Arcturus	...	XII „	XVI	„	„	„
12	Altair ...	...	XVI „	XX	„	„	„
13	Pegasus...	...	XX „	0	„	„	„

Southern Regions

14	Fomalhaut	...	XXII to	II	$-20°$ to $-65°$		
15	Eridanus	...	II „	VI	„	„	„
16	Canopus	...	VI „	X	„	„	„
17	Southern Cross...		X „	XIV	„	„	„
18	Centaur...	...	XIV „ XVIII		„	„	„
19	Sagittarius	...	XVIII „ XXII		„	„	„
20	South Pole	...			$-65°$ „	$-90°$	

Betelgeuze which was on the upper side of the constellation as he viewed it from the Northern Hemisphere is now on the lower side of the constellation, while Rigel which originally appeared on the lower side of Orion is now presented on the upper side. Further Sirius which had stood to the left of Orion while the observer faced south in the Northern Hemisphere will be found on the right side of Orion when the observer has to face north in the Southern Hemisphere. Thus the map of Orion which is correct for an observer in the Southern Hemisphere must be hung upside down to make it correct for an observer in the Northern Hemisphere. Hence we see the reason for the difference between the Regions of the Equatorial zone as presented in the Northern map and the same regions as presented in the Southern map.

We have here assumed that in whichever hemisphere the beginner may be placed he already knows the constellation Orion, for it is the most magnificent constellation in the heavens. If he knows it he will speedily identify the neighbouring bright stars and constellations from their representations on the map.

The beginner in the Northern Hemisphere will probably know also Ursa Major (which perhaps he calls the Great Bear or the Plough or the Dipper). From this as a base the Northern map will easily guide him to acquaintance with other celestial groups of stars. If the beginner is a resident in the Southern Hemisphere he doubtless knows the Southern Cross (Crux). The Southern map will then enable him to make out the names of the various objects in that part of the heavens.

But even if the beginner does not already know any of the constellations, we have now to show how the Northern map or the Southern map may guide him to a knowledge of the principal stars and constellations visible from wherever he may happen to be. If he is in the Northern

Hemisphere the Northern map will generally suffice. If he is in the Southern Hemisphere the Southern map will generally suffice. If he is in or near the tropical parts of the earth he will probably need both maps.

§ 187. Setting the map for the observer's meridian. To avail himself to the fullest extent of either map the observer must first ascertain the position on the map of his meridian at the moment of observation. That depends upon the sidereal time of which an approximate knowledge is sufficient. This can be obtained from the table given on p. 186. The use of this table can be best explained by taking a few examples.

1. It is 9.30 p.m. local mean time in January, what is the nearest hour of sidereal time?

We look in the table under the column headed 9 p.m. to 10 p.m. and in the row marked "Jan." We thus find V which is the nearest hour of sidereal time.

2. It is 3.45 a.m. local mean time in November. We look in the column headed 3 a.m. to 4 a.m. The last row but one corresponds to November and we have VII as the nearest hour of sidereal time.

3. It is 11 p.m. local mean time in May. Here the column headed 10 p.m. to 11 p.m. gives XIV and the column headed 11 p.m. to 12 p.m. gives XV. In such cases we always take the latter because when making out the stars a few minutes later there could be no doubt that XV is right.

4. It is 5.30 a.m. local mean time in June, but daylight having made the maps useless it is unnecessary for our purpose to give any indication of the sidereal time.

The hours 0, I, XXIII *are marked round the margin of each of the maps*, they show the right ascensions (p. 20) of stars on the corresponding meridians. It will be remembered that when a star is on the meridian the sidereal time and the right ascension of the star are the same. For example the line joining the point XVI on the margin of

SIDEREAL TIME TABLE

Local mean time / Date	4 p.m. to 5 p.m.	5 p.m. to 6 p.m.	6 p.m. to 7 p.m.	7 p.m. to 8 p.m.	8 p.m. to 9 p.m.	9 p.m. to 10 p.m.	10 p.m. to 11 p.m.	11 p.m. to mid-night	mid-night to 1 a.m.	1 a.m. to 2 a.m.	2 a.m. to 3 a.m.	3 a.m. to 4 a.m.	4 a.m. to 5 a.m.	5 a.m. to 6 a.m.	6 a.m. to 7 a.m.	7 a.m. to 8 a.m.
Jan.	0	I	II	III	IV	V	VI	VII	VIII	IX	X	XI	XII	XIII	XIV	XV
Feb.	—	III	IV	V	VI	VII	VIII	IX	X	XI	XII	XIII	XIV	XV	XVI	—
Mar.	—	V	VI	VII	VIII	IX	X	XI	XII	XIII	XIV	XV	XVI	XVII	XVIII	—
April	—	—	—	IX	X	XI	XII	XIII	XIV	XV	XVI	XVII	XVIII	—	—	—
May	—	—	—	XI	XII	XIII	XIV	XV	XVI	XVII	XVIII	XIX	XX	—	—	—
June	—	—	—	—	—	XV	XVI	XVII	XVIII	XIX	XX	—	—	—	—	—
July	—	—	—	—	—	XVII	XVIII	XIX	XX	XXI	XXII	—	—	—	—	—
Aug.	—	—	—	XVII	XVIII	XIX	XX	XXI	XXII	XXIII	0	I	II	—	—	—
Sept.	—	—	—	XIX	XX	XXI	XXII	XXIII	0	I	II	III	IV	—	—	—
Oct.	—	XIX	XX	XXI	XXII	XXIII	0	I	II	III	IV	V	VI	VII	VIII	—
Nov.	—	XXI	XXII	XXIII	0	I	II	III	IV	V	VI	VII	VIII	IX	X	—
Dec.	XXII	XXIII	0	I	II	III	IV	V	VI	VII	VIII	IX	X	XI	XII	XIII

the Northern map to the North Pole passes near the bright star Regulus which shows that the right ascension of Regulus is about X. On the Southern map it is seen that a line from the South Pole through Canopus meets the circumference between VI and VII. The right ascension of Canopus is therefore between VI and VII.

The meridian of the observer as represented on either map is found by drawing through the pole at the centre the diameter which terminates at that point of the circumference on which the sidereal time is marked. For instance at 9.30 p.m. in January the observer's meridian on either map is indicated with sufficient accuracy by the diameter joining V and XVII.

§ 188. How to use the maps. We shall suppose the observer is in the open air at night when the sky is clear and preferably when the moon is absent. His first task is to identify that particular one of the six equatorial regions which is visible on his meridian at the moment. The observer should be seated at a desk on which lies the map illumined by a shaded lamp. He is to face south if he is in Europe or North America and using the Northern map. He is to face north if he is in South Africa, Australia or New Zealand and using the Southern map.

After finding the sidereal time by p. 186 from the known local mean time he is *to adjust the map so that the sidereal time as marked on the margin of the map shall be the nearest point of the map to himself.*

1. An observer in London or Toronto or Winnipeg wants to place the map for comparison with the heavens at 8.45 p.m. local mean time in March.

The sidereal time table shows that the sidereal hour is VIII. The observer seats himself looking due south and turns the Northern map on his desk so that the number VIII on its margin is the nearest part of the map to himself.

Region 9 on the map is thus close to the observer. It represents that part of the heavens which stretches from the horizon directly in front of him halfway up towards the zenith. Thus No. 9 is the equatorial region now on his meridian. The map shows that the exceptionally brilliant Star is Sirius in Canis Major, the bright star higher up than Sirius and nearly on the meridian is Procyon. To the right of the line from Sirius to Procyon is the constellation of Orion. Still higher the meridian enters Region 4 in which are Castor and Pollux the bright stars in Gemini. To the right of Gemini lies Auriga with the lustrous Capella. Looking to his left the observer sees Leo in Region 10 and Ursa Major lies between Leo and the North Pole.

2. An observer in Australia wants to name the stars he sees at 11.15 p.m. in October.

He places his chair so that he faces due North. As the hour is between 11 p.m. and midnight the first line of the sidereal time table refers him to the 9th column and in this opposite to October he finds the number I. He is thus instructed to place the Southern map on his desk before him in such a way that I on the circumference of the map is the nearest point of the map to himself; the map is then properly adjusted.

From the part of the map nearest to him he sees that Region 8 is on his meridian and that Aries in Region 8 and Pegasus in Region 13 are near the horizon to right and left of the meridian. Directly in front of him the meridian passes through Cetus. Higher up the meridian enters Region 14 with the 1st magnitude stars Fomalhaut on his left and Achernar on his right. Phoenix is on his meridian and two bright stars in Grus will receive attention. He will also be able to identify objects in Regions 9, 12, 15, 19, 20 and below the pole in Regions 16, 17, 18, though some of them will not be favourably placed.

3. An observer stationed between Ottawa and Vancouver wants to find the names of the stars visible at 2.45 a.m. in July.

The sidereal time table gives sidereal hour XXII; this shows that XXII is the point on the margin of the Northern map which should be nearest the observer as he sits facing south with the map in front of him.

The Region 13 is the nearest to the observer on the map and that equatorial region is consequently the lower part of the heavens immediately in front of him. The constellations Capricornus and Aquarius lie on his meridian and unless he is very far to the North he will see Fomalhaut in Region 14 (for which he will have to consult the Southern map).

Above Aquarius he will note Delphin on his right and the Great Square of Pegasus on his left, and still higher up Cygnus will be on the right and Cassiopeia on the left.

4. An observer in Natal wants to find the names of the stars visible at 3.30 a.m. in February.

The sidereal time table shows the sidereal time to be XIII. The observer now facing north sets the Southern map before him so that the number XIII is the part of the map nearest to him.

Directly in front of the observer Region 11 extends from the horizon upwards. Spica in Virgo will be noticed as the bright star a little to the right of the meridian. Above Virgo is Corvus and then across a wide tract of Centaurus the observer sees Crux or the Southern Cross. In Region 20 near the South Pole the clouds of Magellan will be found : they are visible from every part of the Southern Hemisphere. Scorpio and other fine groups will be seen to the right in Region 18.

5. An observer in Quebec or Montreal or Egypt desires to know when Orion will be in the best situation for observation at 10 p.m.

The Northern map shows that V is the sidereal time when Orion comes on the meridian, *i.e.* the right ascension of Orion. The sidereal time table shows that the conditions desired will be attained at 10 p.m. in January.

6. An observer in New Zealand or Tasmania sees a brilliant star on his meridian at 1.30 a.m. in August. Find the name of that star.

The sidereal time table refers him to XXIII; this must be nearly the right ascension of the star. Looking at the Southern map he sees that the brightest star on the line from XXIII to the South Pole is Fomalhaut. This is accordingly the star he desires to know.

7. In what month will an observer at Cape Town see Alpha Centauri on the meridian about midnight?

The Southern map shows that Alpha Centauri has the right ascension XV to the nearest hour. This proves that May is the month required, for the sidereal time table tells us that XV is the sidereal time at midnight in that month.

8. An observer in Uganda or in other equatorial regions desires to use the maps to identify the stars he sees at 9.30 p.m. in August.

From the sidereal time table he finds the sidereal time to be XIX. As the observer is near the Equator he will need both the Northern and the Southern maps.

To the Equatorial observer the North Pole will lie on the horizon and the Equator will be a great circle passing through his zenith. Aquila will be nearly overhead because it lies on the Equator and its R.A. is nearly XIX and Cygnus lies between Aquila and the point of the horizon which contains the pole star. Far to the west is Boötes and to the east is the Great Square of Pegasus.

The observer being so near the Equator now looks at the Southern map. The South Pole is near the southern horizon, Aquila is overhead and between that and the South Pole is Sagittarius and then the meridian passes between Indus on the east and Scorpio and Ara on the west. Further to the east lie Grus and Fomalhaut and further to the west are Lupus and Centaurus.

9. An observer in Ceylon sees Orion near his zenith between 7 and 8 p.m. in February. Find the constellations visible between Orion and the north, east, west and south points of his horizon.

The sidereal time table shows the sidereal time to be V. The Northern map shows that Auriga is directly between Orion and the North Pole, which is then near the horizon. The Equator extends from the belt of Orion down to the east point through Canis Minor and Hydra and from the Belt of Orion to the West point through Cetus. The Southern map shows the meridian going to the South point through Lepus, Columba and Dorado.

10. At what times may the Pleiades be observed near the meridian?

The Northern map shows that the Right ascension of the Pleiades is between III and IV; the sidereal time table then shows that the Pleiades must be near the meridian in January at 8 p.m., February 6 p.m., September 4 a.m., October 2 a.m., November midnight, December 10 p.m.

REGION I[1]. THE POLE STAR.

The Pole Star or Polaris is looked for by the help of the two stars known as the "Pointers" in Ursa Major (see Region 5). The line drawn from Beta Ursae Majoris to Alpha Ursae Majoris and continued about five times as

[1] It should be stated that the Northern and Southern maps have been based on the series of plates contained in the author's *Popular Guide to the Heavens* (G. Philip and Son). In this work a detailed star chart of each one of the 20 Regions will be found. The positions of each of the planets are also shown for every month from 1910 up to the end of 1950 A.D.

far, will end near the Pole Star which cannot be mistaken, for there is no other bright star in the neighbourhood.

When Polaris has been identified the actual position of the North Pole of the heavens may be obtained as follows. A line drawn from Polaris to Zeta Ursae Majoris the last star but one in the tail of Ursa Major will pass through the Pole. The actual distance from Polaris to the Pole is a degree and a quarter and this is one fourth of the distance between the pointers which are five degrees apart. Thus the pointers not only show the Pole Star but they also provide a scale from which to judge the distance of the Pole from the Pole Star.

Like every other star the Pole Star appears to describe a circle round the Pole in consequence of the Diurnal Motion though owing to its proximity to the Pole the actual circle described by Polaris is very small. Without attentive observation the diurnal motion of Polaris would escape notice. The apparent fixity of the Pole Star makes it a convenient approximate mark to show northward direction.

The distance of Polaris from the Earth is so great that the light it sends us though travelling at the rate of 186,000 miles a second requires at least 63 years to accomplish its journey.

Polaris is a star of the second magnitude. It is attended by a companion star so faint as to be quite invisible to the naked eye. This companion is between the 9th and 10th magnitude so that it requires a telescope of moderate power. The angular distance from Polaris to its companion is about 19″ and their relative position does not seem to undergo any change.

The constellation Ursa Minor contains two other fairly bright stars, namely Beta and Gamma, often called "The Guards." The observer will note how the Guards seem to swing round the Pole Star which appears so nearly fixed and lies at the end of the tail of the Little Bear.

The constellation Cepheus contains three stars of the 3rd magnitude of which two, namely, Beta and Gamma, are in Region 1, while the third, Alpha, is in Region 7. This constellation is chiefly interesting for the possession of the star often known as the Garnet Star. It seems to be the reddest star visible to the naked eye in the Heavens. The Garnet Star will be found in Region 7 as a star of the 5th magnitude. It lies about 5° from Alpha Cephei on the line to Alpha Andromedae which it will be observed is one corner of the great Square of Pegasus (Region 2).

The constellation Draco winds through Region 1, but its most interesting parts are in Region 6.

REGION 2. CASSIOPEIA.

If the line of pointers from Ursa Major to the Pole Star be produced as far again the extremity of the line will be close to Cassiopeia. The principal stars of this constellation will be easily recognised as they form a large W.

The extreme star on the right of Cassiopeia is known as Beta Cassiopeiae and the next star to it in the configuration is Alpha Cassiopeiae.

The line from Beta through Alpha produced about four times as far indicates the star Gamma Andromedae which is one of the most beautiful of all double stars. The largest star of the pair is a topaz colour and the smaller is of an emerald hue. If the telescope is unusually good the emerald star may itself be shown to be composed of two stars.

A line from Gamma Andromedae to the nearest corner of the Great Square of Pegasus passes about half way the second magnitude star Beta Andromedae. From this the position of a very important object can be indicated, for a point one fourth of the way from Beta Andromedae towards Beta Cassiopeiae will be close to the great Nebula in Andromeda. This is the only Nebula which can be discerned with the unaided eye. The telescope or better still the photographic plate is needed to bring out the full importance of this mighty object, see pp. 163, 164 and plate facing p. 164.

While in Region 2 we must also note Alpha Arietis, the brightest star in the first of the Signs of the Zodiac. Aries was the constellation which did actually contain the vernal equinoctial point (p. 18) centuries ago. But this fundamental point is in continual motion. Its present position may be indicated by the following construction. When the Great Square of Pegasus is toward the South imagine the left vertical side produced downwards to a distance equal to its own length; from the point thus found imagine a line drawn to the West, parallel to the lower horizontal side of the square and one fifth of its length. This terminates near the present position of the "first point of Aries"; as the equinoctial point is still termed though it has now entered the constellation Pisces.

REGION 3. CAPELLA.

The Milky Way here sweeps over the constellation Auriga adorned by a notable star of the first magnitude Alpha Aurigae generally known as Capella.

Capella is easily identified as the bright star which lies half way between the Belt of Orion and the Pole Star. It may also be noticed that Capella lies nearly in line with the largest side of the quadrilateral figure forming part of Ursa Major.

As Vega (see Region 7) is the star characteristic of summer nights so Capella is the star characteristic of winter nights. Capella comes to the meridian at midnight in the beginning of December and is then only about 6° south of the zenith of London.

Capella may be also identified by the narrow isosceles triangle of three small stars which lies near it. These three stars according to ancient fancy are known as Haedi the "kids," Capella itself being the "goat."

The lustre of Capella is not quite so great as that of Vega. In some other respects these two great stars are analogous. They each have a small proper motion amounting to about a third of a second per annum. Vega and Capella are nearly equally distant from the Earth being about 1,700,000 times as far as the Sun.

One point of contrast between the two great Northern stars may be mentioned. Vega is one of those intensely white stars like Sirius which contain indication of a great atmosphere of hydrogen. Capella is rather a star of the type to which the Sun itself belongs. In this respect Capella resembles Alpha Centauri (Region 18) and Arcturus (Region 6).

Capella and Vega are brighter than any other stars in the Northern Hemisphere. In the Southern Hemisphere, however, Sirius, Canopus and Alpha Centauri are all more brilliant than Vega or Capella.

Capella is a remarkable binary star (p. 169). It is a pair of brilliant suns so close together that it is not likely that any telescope will ever enable them to be seen separately. It requires a spectroscope to show that the light from the star comes from two contiguous but distinct sources. One of these stars revolves round the other in 104 days. This beautiful discovery was made independently by Professor Newall at Cambridge and by Professor Campbell at the Lick Observatory, California. As the light from this pair of stars takes about 27 years to reach the Earth we see that at any moment the full particulars of 90 complete revolutions must be on their way.

13—2

Beta Aurigae is nearly on the same parallel as Capella and south of Capella is another second magnitude star Beta Tauri. The three form an isosceles triangle each of the two equal sides being twice as long as the third side.

The line from Beta Aurigae through Capella produced three times as far indicates Algol the famous variable. In each period of $2\frac{3}{4}$ days Algol goes through a series of changes by descending from the second magnitude to the fourth and then ascending again to the second.

North of Algol across a branch of the Milky Way is the fine star Alpha Persei. There are two famous clusters of stars in the same constellation discernible by the naked eye and unspeakably magnificent in a large telescope (see p. 160 and plate opposite).

Region 4. Gemini.

The constellation Cancer contains only unimportant stars. It is however characterised by a curious star cluster known as Praesepe, the Beehive, which is quite visible to the unaided eye. Praesepe will be easily identified as the hazy looking spot between Gemini and Leo. With the slightest telescopic assistance such as is afforded by an opera glass Praesepe is resolved into stars.

The constellation Lynx is inconspicuous though like every other part of the heavens it contains many double stars and other objects interesting to the possessor of a good telescope[1].

The most important objects in Region 4 are the two bright stars of Gemini universally known as Castor and Pollux. It is generally admitted that Castor enjoys the distinction of being the finest binary star (p. 169) in the Northern Heavens. Fortunately this splendid object is

---

[1] Reference may be made to that excellent book for observers in the northern hemisphere, Webb's *Celestial Objects for Common Telescopes*.

within the reach of telescopes quite moderate in power. The two components of Castor are of the second and third magnitude respectively and they are separated by a distance of 5″. One of these stars is in revolution about the other. But the movement is slow. Over a century has been required for the line joining the components to rotate through 90° and the motion is not uniform.

Spectroscopic investigation has shown that the movements of the two bright stars seem to be complicated by the presence of dark masses in the vicinity whose attractions disturb the comparatively simple movements that would otherwise have been expected.

REGION 5. URSA MAJOR.

The most conspicuous group of stars in Region 5 is the constellation of Ursa Major. The seven stars are marked consecutively Alpha, Beta, Gamma, Delta, Epsilon, Zeta, Eta. Of these Zeta otherwise called Mizar is a favourite telescopic object. Of all the double stars in the heavens Mizar requires the smallest amount of telescopic assistance.

Coma Berenices is a gathering of faint stars not dense enough to be called a cluster.

Canes Venatici contains the fine double star Cor Caroli. This object is easily found from the stars of Ursa Major by joining Alpha to Gamma and then producing the joining line one and a half times farther. Another method of finding it is given by Admiral Smyth. With the sweep of the Bear's Tail as the top of a flying kite the end of the tail of the kite is marked by Cor Caroli. The geometer will note that Cor Caroli and the three stars of the Bear's Tail form a quadrilateral such as could be inscribed in a circle.

Cor Caroli is a star of the third magnitude and its companion at a distance of 20″ is between the fifth and the sixth magnitude. It is thus a very easy object for the telescope. As the two stars have a common proper motion it seems evident that they belong to the same system though motion of revolution has not yet been observed.

But the most remarkable object in Canes Venatici is the spiral nebula discovered by Lord Rosse in 1845. This nebula is best shown in photographs for even the greatest telescopes cannot display the spiral structure so clearly as it is obtained in a photograph. Through small telescopes little is to be seen except two nebulae very close together. The famous Parsonstown reflector revealed to Lord Rosse the spiral whorls uniting these nebulae.

Though the great Spiral is quite invisible to the naked eye yet it is worth while to point out its locality in Region 5. Imagine a line drawn from Eta at the end of the tail of Ursa Major one fourth of the way to Cor Caroli: the point thus indicated shows where the great Spiral is to be looked for.

It is now believed that spiral nebulae are scattered over the heavens in such profusion that they must be reckoned in hundreds of thousands. Next to the fixed stars themselves spiral nebulae are the most characteristic constituents of the sidereal heavens.

REGION 6. HERCULES.

The constellation Hercules lies chiefly in Region 6 but a part of it which includes its brightest star Alpha Herculis must be sought in Region 12. It there serves as one of the corners of the quadrangle characteristic of Ophiuchus. Alpha Herculis is a beautiful double star with components of finely contrasted colours one being of an orange hue while the other is bluish-green.

Nearly midway between the stars Zeta and Eta in Hercules lies the superb globular cluster of which a photograph is shown in the plate facing p. 159. This object is faintly visible to the naked eye on a very dark night.

Corona is a pleasing group of stars, between Boötes and Hercules. It is one of the few constellations whose name is justified by its appearance.

Draco is a winding and involved constellation. The bright star Gamma Draconis will be found about one third of the way from Alpha Cygni towards Arcturus. Draco contains the most striking example we have of those curious telescopic objects known as planetary nebulae. It is a small blue globe one third of the way from Gamma Draconis to the Pole Star.

REGION 7. VEGA.

Lyra contains the beautiful first magnitude star Vega or Alpha Lyrae which is easily visible from all parts of the Northern Hemisphere. Indeed Vega rises above the horizon of every station in the world unless the South latitude of that station exceeds · 51°.

As Vega is about 51° from the North Pole it may be observed both at upper and at lower culmination from all stations in the Northern Hemisphere of which the latitude exceeds 51°. Thus Vega at no time goes below the horizon of an observer in the greater part of the British Isles.

There will be no difficulty in identifying this star when Region 7 in the heavens and its representation in the map are compared. It may however be noticed that just as two stars in the quadrangle of the Great Bear form the pointers to the Pole Star so the other two stars of the same quadrangle are the pointers to Vega. The attention of the observer should be directed to the isosceles triangle of which the three corners are respectively the Pole Star, Arcturus, and Vega.

At midnight about the end of June, Vega comes to upper culmination nearly 12° south of the zenith at London. It culminates at 10 p.m. in July and at 8 p.m. in August. It is this which makes Vega the star of the summer night. From September till the following February the upper culmination of Vega takes place in daylight.

Vega is three times as far from the Earth as Sirius, and consequently if Vega were brought to the same distance as Sirius its light would be increased ninefold. Such an exaltation of its lustre would make Vega appear with the actual lustre of Sirius. Thus we may reasonably conjecture that these two superb stars are not only alike in the beauty of their radiant hues and in the indications they present of immense atmospheres of Hydrogen, but they are also alike in their character as suns for the diffusion of light and heat.

The distance of Vega from the earth is indeed so vast that from the time its light leaves the star until it arrives at the earth not less than 27 years have elapsed. As we look at the Star of Summer on a fine evening in the year 1911 we see the brilliant-gem not as it is at the moment, we see it as it was in the year 1884, the light which now enters our eyes has needed all that time for its journey even though it travels 10,000 times as fast as the earth moves in its orbit.

It follows that if Vega were to be struck from existence it would still adorn the summer skies of the Northern Hemisphere for 27 years. Not until all the light that had sped on its way had reached our eyes could we become aware that the star had vanished.

If the Sun and Vega could be placed side by side it would seem that the light emitted by Vega must be 130 times that emitted by the Sun.

Lyra has many further claims to the notice of the astronomer. Let it here suffice to mention that it presents the remarkable double-double star Epsilon and that its ring nebula is the most perfect example known of this remarkable type of object.

Some of the richest parts of the Milky Way traverse

those parts of the heavens included in Region **7.** The first magnitude star Alpha Cygni is the brightest object in Cygnus. The same constellation also contains Beta Cygni an exquisite double star with contrasted colours and fortunately easily identified as the beak of the long outstretched neck of the Swan.

REGION 8. CETUS.

Region 8 is one of the six equatorial regions. It is therefore found both on Maps I and II, as already explained. When Map I is turned round so that Region 11 is nearest the observer it presents Region 8 as it is shown in Map II.

We see from the sidereal time table that Region 8 is on the meridian about 6 p.m. in January. This shows that in the winter months, Region 8 can be well seen soon after darkness sets in. Towards the end of August Region 8 culminates at 4 a.m.; in September at 2 a.m.; in October at midnight; in November at 10 p.m.; and December at 8 p.m.

Cetus is sometimes said to be the largest constellation in the heavens. It is not however made brilliant or conspicuous by the possession of many bright stars. It contains two second magnitude stars and nine of the third and fourth magnitudes. Admiral Smyth advises observers to note the gigantic W of which Alpha Ceti and Alpha Arietis form the lower points while Aldebaran the Pleiades and Beta Persei mark the upper points.

The wonderful variable star known as Mira Ceti lies in Cetus. For more than three hundred years it has been known that Mira Ceti exhibits extraordinary fluctuations of brightness. Its changes take place in a period of about eleven months. From being a small telescopic star of the ninth magnitude Mira slowly brightens up to the eighth, seventh, sixth, magnitude in succession after which it becomes visible to the naked eye and gradually ascends to the second magnitude. Indeed it is recorded that on one occasion the lustre of Mira rivalled that of the first magnitude star Aldebaran. Its maximum in each periodic group of changes is reached about four months after the rise commences. The star continues at its maximum for nearly a month and then the decline begins. Slowly the brightness wanes until in five months more Mira has returned to the insignificant telescopic star of the ninth magnitude from which it started.

Justly is this star called *Mira* Ceti for the light that it yields when at its maximum is quite 1500 times that given when at its minimum.

Taurus is specially noteworthy for its bright star Aldebaran and for the interesting group known since ancient days as the Pleiades.

REGION 9. SIRIUS.

The splendid star Sirius is, beyond all comparison, the brightest luminary that is truly a star. It is so placed that it can be seen at suitable seasons from the greater part of the earth. Sirius is a glorious object from whatever point in the Southern Hemisphere the observer may view it. Watchers of the skies are equally fortunate in most parts of the Northern Hemisphere. It is only a resident within the Arctic regions who would not enjoy the privilege of seeing Sirius to some extent.

The great star has a South Declination of 16° and it comes on the meridian at midnight in the beginning of January. It follows that residents in a South latitude of 16°, for example in the Kimberley division of Western Australia, in the Northern Territory of South Australia or in the Cape York Peninsula of Queensland will have Sirius at the zenith, *i.e.* directly overhead, at midnight about Christmas time. The same may be stated with regard to Rhodesia. In a more Northerly part of Africa than

Rhodesia, for example Egypt, Sirius would not pass directly overhead, it would lie to the South but of course much higher than it is when viewed from Great Britain. In a more Southerly part of Africa than Rhodesia, say for example at the Cape of Good Hope, Sirius would appear rather to the North. Sirius has a Right Ascension between VI and VII so that from p. 186 we see it comes on the meridian about 9 p.m. in February.

The Sun and the Moon, the planets Venus and Jupiter, and perhaps an occasional comet are the only celestial bodies which surpass Sirius in splendour. It has been stated on good authority that Sirius has been seen by the unaided eye during bright sunshine. ·The like statement cannot be made with regard to any other star though the planet Venus when at its best is easily to be so detected. Many observers have seen Venus at 2.30 in the afternoon of a beautiful June day without any optical aid whatever.

It may be useful to note that an observer in the Northern Hemisphere will find Sirius indicated by following the line of the three stars in the Belt of Orion to the left. They point as unmistakably to Sirius as the pointers in the Great Bear point to the Pole star.

An observer at Cape Town or anywhere else in the Southern Temperate region will also find Sirius by the three stars in the Belt of Orion, but in his latitudes he will look to the right of Orion instead of to the left as we do in the Northern Hemisphere. The reason for this has been already explained on p. 183.

Sirius is the principal object in the not otherwise re- markable constellation known as Canis Major. From the time of Homer down to the present day Sirius itself is often called the Dog star. Sirius is indicated by a dog in various Egyptian monuments. Its rising at the same time as the sun in mid-summer was anciently supposed to be connected with the beginning of the inundations of the Nile[1].

Sirius has always been a fascinating star if it were only from its beautiful scintillation of colours. The Dog star is indeed a typically and intensely white star but the twinkling which it displays in such a marked degree causes it to flash forth varied tints in rapid succession.

As might be expected from its exceptional splendour Sirius is one of the nearest of the stars to the earth. It is nevertheless about 560,000 times as far from us as is the sun, and the light from Sirius takes $8\frac{1}{2}$ years to reach the earth. It is impossible to doubt that if we were as near to Sirius as we are to the Sun the splendour of Sirius would be seen to exceed greatly that of the Sun.

The surpassing lustre of Sirius as compared with other stars also ranked of the first magnitude may be realized from the fact that Sirius sends to the Earth eleven times as much light as does Aldebaran the brightest star in the constellation of the "Bull." This may be borne in mind when we are viewing Sirius and Aldebaran symmetrically placed on opposite sides of the Belt of Orion. Though Sirius appears constantly in the same region of the heavens so far as mere eye observations are concerned, yet when careful measurement of its position is made with accurate instruments the great star is seen to be in motion and in rapid motion too as measured by ordinary terrestrial standards. Sirius has a stately progress through space at the average rate of 1000 miles a minute. Observation showed that the velocity with which the star urges its way was not strictly constant. The fluctuations in its velocity which were measured admitted of only one explanation. They required that there must be another star

[1] See *Star Names and their Meanings*, by R. H. Allen, p. 123 (G. E. Stechert and Co., New York and London). This work is full of interesting information and curious lore.

or body of some kind in the vicinity of Sirius and that the attraction of this other body disturbed the motion of Sirius. This other body was subsequently revealed by observation. It was, as might have been expected, indeed a star, but how different was this disturbing companion star from Sirius itself. In mere weight there is no doubt disparity between the two bodies. The companion of Sirius is about one-half the weight of Sirius itself; this will however hardly prepare us for the undoubted fact that the companion does not possess one five thousandth part of the lustre of Sirius. The companion is sun-like in its mass but not at all sun-like in its splendour. This dull companion and the glorious orb revolve each around the other in a period of 52 years and the two stars have together a weight about $5\frac{1}{2}$ times as great as the weight of the Sun.

On pp. 182–3 we have given a general description of the great constellation of Orion the most characteristic feature of Region 9 as seen from either the Northern or the Southern Hemisphere. We now add some account of important stars in this region.

On a clear January night about 10 o'clock the observer in the Northern Hemisphere looking Southwards has as already explained the constellation of Orion directly before him. A little to the right of the Belt of Orion and below it is the first magnitude star Rigel or Beta Orionis. The telescope shows a small blue star close to Rigel, the two being evidently associated by their mutual attraction. It should always be remembered that Rigel is one of four first magnitude stars forming a remarkable lozenge-shaped figure. The other three stars are Sirius, Betelgeuze and Aldebaran and the Belt of Orion is the centre of the lozenge.

Rigel is one of those stars sufficiently near the Equator to be easily seen from almost all parts of the inhabited world. It would be right overhead at midnight in early

December to any observer in the northerly part of North Eastern Rhodesia or at Pernambuco in Brazil.

The first magnitude star Procyon in the constellation of the Lesser Dog comes on the meridian about 2 a.m. in the middle of December. Procyon will easily be recognised by carrying on to the left the line of the two stars Bellatrix and Betelgeuze which form the uppermost side of the quadrangle of Orion. It should be noted that the brilliant stars Castor and Pollux of the constellation Gemini lie on the line between Procyon and the Pole star.

Vertically below the middle star of the Belt of Orion is the Swordhandle which contains the great nebula in Orion one of the greatest celestial objects for the telescope (p. 163).

The declination of Procyon being 5° 29′ we find that it will culminate in the zenith of an observer a few degrees north of the Equator. It will be visible in January during night time from nearly every part of the world. At the Cape of Good Hope for example Procyon culminates at midnight in January at an altitude of almost 50°.

Procyon is a double star for associated with it is a telescopic companion which offers a remarkable contrast. Procyon is a bright star but the companion is a very faint star, in fact it has been shown that the light from Procyon is 4700 times greater than that which comes from its companion. But there is another point to be noticed; the mass of the companion is very much greater than would be thought from this statement. It appears that Procyon is only about seven times as heavy as its companion. We are thus reminded of Sirius (p. 205).

These facts illustrate the important principle that the lustre of stars and their masses bear no obvious relation. In all probability there are stars invisible because they give no appreciable light but which have masses rivalling those of the greatest visible stars.

REGION 10. REGULUS.

The pointers in the Great Bear which we use to indicate the Pole Star will also help to find the constellation Leo. The line through the pointers which in one direction leads to the Pole Star will in the opposite direction lead to Leo, and Leo is about as far on one side of the pointers as the Pole Star is on the other. The group of stars which form the important zodiacal constellation of Leo have a remarkable configuration. The lucida of the group is a star of the first magnitude known as Alpha Leonis or more usually as Regulus, and Regulus is the first of a notable curve of stars forming the head of the Lion and often known by the designation of the "Sickle." The rest of the constellation extends from the convex side of the Sickle to terminate in the second magnitude star Denebola which marks the end of the tail of the Lion.

Leo is one of the constellations through which the Sun appears to pass in its annual circuit of the heavens. It thus happens that on each 21st August the Sun is close to Regulus. The second brightest star in the Sickle will be easily identified in the curve from Regulus. It is known as Gamma Leonis, and is a good example of an easy telescopic double star. The larger of the two components is of the second magnitude and the smaller is of the fourth magnitude and three seconds distant. There is an interesting contrast between the hues of the two components. It may be a useful aid to the memory to note that Aldebaran, Gamma Geminorum, Gamma Leonis and Denebola are lying nearly on a great circle.

In the centre of the Sickle is the radiant point from which the magnificent shower of shooting stars diverged in November, 13—14, 1866. This shower returns with more or less regularity and whenever it does so it is referred to as a display of the Leonids.

REGION 11. ARCTURUS.

Boötes (Region 6) is chiefly famous for the possession of the first magnitude star Arcturus. The most remarkable occasion on which this star was ever observed must have been the 5th October, 1858. The brilliant Arcturus was then seen right through the splendid Comet of Donati and appeared with hardly diminished lustre, though it approached the nucleus of the comet so closely as to be only 20′ distant.

No bright star in the heavens is more easy to identify than Arcturus. It is only necessary to look for Ursa Major, follow the sweep of the tail of the Bear for a little less than twice its length and then the eye is conducted to Arcturus.

Arcturus comes on the meridian at midnight in the latter part of April being then about 30° south of the zenith to an observer in England. In May it culminates about 10 p.m. For Arcturus to culminate in the zenith it would be necessary for the observer to be within the tropics. It culminates very near the zenith in Suakin or Dongola and the same may be said of the North of Hayti or the South of Cuba. On the Equator Arcturus culminates about 20° to the north of the zenith. It culminates a little to the north of the zenith at Bombay and a little to the south at Mandalay. With increasing southern latitudes the altitude at culmination decreases but not until a South latitude about 70° was reached could it be said that Arcturus had become invisible. It may therefore be stated as approximately true that Arcturus is visible from all parts of the Earth except within the Antarctic circle.

Arcturus is five times as remote from the Earth as either Vega or Capella, and since it appears as bright as either of these stars we infer that Arcturus must have 25 times the splendour of either Vega or Capella. The light-giving power of Arcturus has been estimated to be 1300 times that of the Sun.

Arcturus is also remarkable for its large proper motion which carries it across the heavens through an arc of 2″·1 yearly. The annual parallax of this star is 0″·024 and we therefore infer that the actual speed with which Arcturus is wending its way cannot be less than 280 miles per second.

It is said that Arcturus is the first star to have been observed in the day time with a telescope. It has even been seen with the unaided eye before the Sun has set.

The constellation Virgo has as its most conspicuous feature the first magnitude star called Spica or Alpha Virginis. If a line joining Alpha Ursae Majoris to Gamma Ursae Majoris be prolonged with a slight curve it will lead to Spica. The observer should then note that three fine stars Arcturus, Spica, and Denebola make a nearly equilateral triangle. To one who desires to obtain a knowledge of the stars the perception of large configurations like this is often helpful.

The constellation Serpens will be identified by its brightest star Alpha Serpentis which lies to the left of Arcturus. Corvus will be noted a little below Spica to the right, and the two bright stars Beta Corvi and Gamma Corvi form with Spica an isosceles triangle.

REGION 12. ALTAIR.

Aquila is characterised by the first magnitude star Altair (Alpha Aquilae). It will assist the student of the stars to note the striking triangle of which the three vertices are Altair, Vega and Deneb or Alpha Cygni (this star must not be confounded with Denebola in the tail of Leo). A line from Vega under Beta Cygni passes near the line of three stars which form the most conspicuous part of Aquila.

B. A.   14

Altair is much the brightest of the row of three stars of which it is the middle one. It is said that very inexperienced star gazers have before now mistaken these three stars for the Belt of Orion. In its celestial wanderings the Milky Way passes across a part of the constellation Aquila. Legend suggests that at this point the celestial Eagle is flying across the celestial river termed the Milky Way[1].

It is interesting to record that the first comet ever discovered by the camera from the trail it left on a photographic plate was found by Professor E. E. Barnard on 12th October, 1892, in the constellation Aquila.

The three leading stars of Ophiuchus form with Alpha Herculis an irregular quadrangle at almost the same declination as Altair.

REGION 13. SQUARE OF PEGASUS.

Lying partly in Region 2 and partly in Regions 8 and 13 is that remarkable celestial figure the Great Square of Pegasus. A knowledge of this configuration is as useful for the student of the stars in the Northern Hemisphere, as is the knowledge of Centaurus for the student in the Southern Hemisphere and the constellation of Orion for the student of both Hemispheres. Three of the stars in the Great Square are lettered a, β, γ Pegasi and do no doubt belong to the constellation Pegasus but the fourth star has been, from time immemorial, reckoned as one of the stars of the adjacent constellation Andromeda in which it is lettered a.

The Great Square is conveniently indicated by a line from the Pole star through Beta Cassiopeiae thus reaching Alpha Andromedae.

[1] For the interesting legend of the Spinning Damsel and much other quaint lore about Aquila, see *Star Names and their Meanings*, by R. H. Allen, p. 58.

About 30 stars can be counted in the interior of the Great Square by an observer in the latitude of Great Britain using only his unaided eyes, but in purer Southern skies a considerably greater number can be seen. An observer in Athens has reckoned 102.

Delphin is a small group, which is pointed out by the lower side of the Great Square continued to the right for a distance equal to twice the side of the Square. There are no stars in Delphin brighter than the third magnitude, but of these there are five, four of which form a small rhomboid that when once identified will be easily remembered.

To the left of Delphin and a little below is Epsilon Pegasi of the second magnitude. This star if moved a short distance to the right would equally divide a line from Delphin to another remarkable little asterism in Aquarius. These form a triangle of stars with another star Zeta Aquarii in the inside. Zeta is a fine double star, the components of which are of magnitudes 4 and $4\frac{1}{2}$.

Aquarius may also be identified by the line from Vega to Delphin if continued as far again.

REGION 14. FOMALHAUT.

This Region is of much interest as it contains one of the brightest parts of the Southern heavens. We there find the two first magnitude stars Alpha Eridani or Achernar and Alpha Piscis Australis or Fomalhaut.

Piscis Australis lies to the South of Pisces and Aquarius. It is a small collection of stars containing Fomalhaut as its only conspicuous object. The line from Fomalhaut to Achernar carried on for an equal distance in the same direction will reach the brilliant Canopus. We have here a remarkable case, which should be specially attended to, of three first magnitude stars in line. This line will be found to help observers in the Southern

Hemisphere in identifying groups of Southern stars. Only the first of the three, namely Fomalhaut, is visible from Great Britain.

Nearly on the line from Fomalhaut to Achernar and a little more than half way is a star of the second magnitude called Alpha Phoenicis, because it is the lucida of the constellation Phoenix. The remaining stars in this little constellation are inconspicuous.

On the left side of the line from Fomalhaut to Achernar lies the constellation of Grus. It contains two second magnitude stars marked Alpha and Beta, and it will be noted that these stars are in line with Alpha Phoenicis. We thus observe that the long line of three first magnitude stars just referred to is crossed by a shorter line of three second magnitude stars.

The constellation Sculptor consists mainly of very small stars. It has however one star Beta of the fourth magnitude which lies nearly midway between Fomalhaut and Alpha Phoenicis. The star Alpha Sculptoris of about equal brightness to Beta lies between Alpha Phoenicis and Cetus.

In the constellation Tucana there are two bright stars Alpha and Beta which as indicated on the map form a noteworthy configuration with Alpha, Beta, and Gamma of the constellation Grus.

REGION 15   ERIDANUS.

The chief feature to be identified in Region 15 is the long celestial river Eridanus which has its origin at Achernar ("The End of the River") and then flows away from the South Pole. The track of Eridanus is indicated by a succession of bright stars. An interesting group of four stars of the fourth and fifth magnitudes may be specially noted. A little further on the river passes a star of the third magnitude after which it winds still further North until it is traced into the Equatorial Region 18.

Above Achernar the course of Eridanus can be followed almost due South into the constellation Hydrus which must be sought in Region 20.

Eridanus is the largest constellation in the heavens. It contains nearly 300 stars bright enough to be visible to the naked eye, though with the exception of Achernar it possesses no star brighter than the third magnitude.

It may be useful to note that the middle point of the line from Achernar to Beta Centauri (Region 17) is very close to the South Pole.

Adjacent to Eridanus is Fornax of which Alpha the brightest star is a very fine double with components of about the fourth and seventh magnitudes. The boundaries of the different constellations in this as in other parts of the heavens are often somewhat ill defined. The star we have just referred to is sometimes described as 12 Eridani and appears thus to be excluded from Fornax.

Dorado (" The Gold fish[1] ") is a line of stars of which one reaches the third magnitude while the remainder are inconsiderable.

Columba should be noticed as a pleasing small triangle of brilliants, two of which are of the third magnitude. A line from Sirius towards Achernar will pass very near Columba at one-third of the distance.

REGION 16. CANOPUS.

The famous constellation Argo Navis, often called simply Argo, is the characteristic feature of Region 16. Owing to the wide extent of Argo it has been found convenient to subdivide the constellation into three others. We thus have Carina the keel, Puppis the stern, and Vela the sails.

[1] Allen, *Star Names and their Meanings*, p. 218.

Nearly on the same meridian as Sirius but 36° nearer to the South Pole shines the glorious Canopus (often known as Alpha Argûs) which is second only to Sirius in its brilliance. It will be noted that neither of these peerless orbs lies in the Northern Hemisphere. Sirius being so much nearer the Equator than Canopus is visible from a much greater extent of the Earth's surface.

When Canopus culminates it just reaches the horizon of any station at the North latitude 37° 20′. To see Canopus the observer should accordingly be in a north latitude some degrees below 37° 20′. This great star is therefore always hidden from every European station. It can however be seen in Winter at Cairo, and as the Nile is ascended this celestial gem appears higher and higher each evening so that it has appropriately been called the star of the Nile. It derives its name Canopus from an ancient sea-port town in Egypt 15 miles North East of Alexandria, which is itself said to have derived its name from Canopus the pilot of the fleet of Menelaus in 1183 B.C.

The two splendid stars of the Southern skies, Sirius and Canopus, can be seen to great advantage in Sydney and Melbourne. In such southern latitudes at Christmas-tide Sirius (see p. 203) and Canopus will come on the meridian at midnight at such high altitudes as will display the stars' brilliance to great advantage. The same may be said of any other place of which the south latitude is about the same, and thus Adelaide, Brisbane and Perth and also Cape Town, Port Elizabeth and Durban are well situated. Such a display of the two most splendid stars as is seen from these favoured localities goes far to justify the belief that the celestial objects in the southern skies are more impressive than those of our northern heavens. Canopus, as well as Sirius, is also well placed for observation from Auckland, Wellington, Christchurch or elsewhere in New Zealand and also from Hobart and Tasmania generally. In the new world Canopus can be seen about Christmas time from latitudes like those of Georgia and Florida southwards.

To see Canopus near the zenith or right overhead, the observer should be in about South latitude 52° : there are but few attainable stations in such latitudes.

At or near Cape Horn the requisite conditions would be found. A navigator passing through the Straits of Magellan at Christmas or shepherds keeping watch in the Falkland Islands would find Canopus right overhead at midnight. At the same time these observers would note Sirius in the North with an altitude of 54°. The greater elevation of Canopus would thus somewhat reduce the superiority of the lustre of Sirius and an interesting comparison of the brightness of the two celestial gems could be made.

Canopus is certainly more than ten times as far from the Earth as is Sirius, and its light requires more than a century to reach the Earth from the moment it left the star. The intrinsic splendour of Canopus must be thousands of times greater than that of the Sun.

REGION 17. THE SOUTHERN CROSS.

This Region is noteworthy as containing two of the most remarkable constellations in the southern heavens, for in it we find both Centaurus and the Southern Cross which is generally marked Crux on the astronomical maps.

The Southern Cross contains a number of bright stars in a comparatively small region. It is generally considered to be as characteristic of the Southern heavens as Ursa Major is of the Northern.

The long dimension of the Southern Cross points nearly to the South Pole and in the other direction the line continued across Centaurus will lead to Beta Corvi. The shorter dimension of the Southern Cross points to that part of the Centaur which contains the magnificent stars which we shall mention in Region 18.

The brightest of the group, known as Alpha Crucis, is the nearest star of the Cross to the South Pole. Alpha Crucis is a Standard first magnitude star of just the same brightness as Aldebaran and more than twice as bright as the Pole Star. When viewed through a telescope Alpha Crucis is seen to be a splendid double star with components nearly equal in magnitude and almost five seconds of arc apart. It is noteworthy that the relative position of the two stars has remained apparently without change since the first observations in 1826. Photographs of the region by Mr H. C. Russell at Sydney showed that Alpha Crucis lies in a remarkable little cluster of extremely faint stars with which the bright star itself is presumably in some physical connection. This is an observation of great interest for it seems to be a unique case.

The most easterly star of the Southern Cross is known as Beta Crucis. An attempt was made by Sir David Gill and Dr Elkin to determine the distance of this star. The result proved that Beta Crucis is so remote that the light which it sends us must take centuries on its journey. To those who have a good telescope it is important to know that close to Beta Crucis is a very curious eighth magnitude star which Sir John Herschel describes as "the fullest and deepest maroon red, the most intense blood-red of any star I have seen. It is like a drop of blood when contrasted with the whiteness of Beta Crucis."

The Southern Cross is traversed by one of the most brilliant parts of that truly wonderful stream of stars the Milky Way (see p. 160). Here is presented one of the most remarkable features in the whole course of the celestial river. The corruscating masses of light are suddenly[1] "interrupted by a pear-shaped black opening eight degrees

[1] I here quote Agnes Clarke, *System of the Stars*, p. 336.

long by five wide, named by early navigators the 'Coal-Sack.' This yawning excavation figures in Australian folk-lore as the embodiment of evil in the shape of an Emu, who lies in wait at the foot of a tree represented by the Stars of the Cross for an opossum driven by his persecutions to take refuge among its branches. The legend reads almost like a Christian parable."

Centaurus is a constellation of vast extent and contains more brilliant gems than any other group in the heavens either North or South. It has two stars of the first magnitude, one of the second, five of the third, seven of the fourth and 39 of the fifth.

The main part of Centaurus which is contained in Region 17 is marked by a winding chain extending from Theta Centauri to Delta Centauri.

In Centaurus is the globular cluster Omega Centauri nearly midway between Theta Centauri and Gamma Crucis. Sir John Herschel says it is "beyond all comparison the richest and largest object of the kind in the heavens." In a powerful telescope it appears as a globe about 20 minutes in diameter of innumerable small stars gradually increasing in brightness towards the centre. It is visible to the naked eye like a star of the fifth magnitude.

REGION 18. ALPHA CENTAURI.

This famous star is characterized by a notable circumstance. It is so far as is known nearer to the Earth than is any other star. Alpha Centauri is only one-half as many miles away from us as is Sirius. But Alpha Centauri is nevertheless at a distance which is 280,000 times as great as that of the Sun. When we look at this star we may reflect that the rays of light now reaching our eyes have taken 4·4 years for their journey from Star to Earth.

Alpha Centauri, the brightest star in the constellation of the Centaur, is within 30° of the South Pole of the

14—5

heavens. A denizen of the Northern Hemisphere will hardly see this star until he approaches the tropics. At Calcutta Alpha Centauri culminates about 7° above the horizon and may be then observed at midnight at the end of April. In Ceylon or elsewhere about the latitude of Colombo, this star can be seen to greater advantage for it culminates at the height of 23°.

An observer in the Southern Hemisphere can have no difficulty in making out Alpha Centauri, since it may be identified by the circumstance that another splendid star Beta Centauri lies within 5° of Alpha. Such a juxta-position of two first magnitude stars is not paralleled in any other part of the heavens. For though the beautiful pair so well known as Castor and Pollux in the Northern Hemisphere are separated by about the same distance, namely 5°, they are not equal in lustre to Alpha and Beta Centauri.

There is no easily accessible station from which Alpha Centauri can ever be seen at the zenith of the observer. This would however be possible to one who resided in the South Shetland Isles about 500 miles south of Cape Horn.

The stars Alpha and Beta Centauri are situated in a remarkable region of the southern heavens. At the same distance from the South Pole lies the famous constellation of the Southern Cross.

When viewed through the telescope Alpha Centauri is seen to be a double star composed of two bright stars so close together that the duplicity cannot be discerned by the unaided eye. The larger of the two components emits three times as much light as the smaller, the two combined have a lustre which is only exceeded by that of Sirius or Canopus. Alpha Centauri is one of those double stars which is properly termed binary and the two components revolve one around the other under the influence of their mutual attraction in a period a little longer than 80 years.

Besides this orbital movement of each component with respect to the others the two stars together have a joint progressive movement by which they advance 3″·7 annually. This is the largest proper motion possessed by any bright star though certain small stars have a greater proper motion. There is for instance one which moves through an arc of 7″ annually and another through an arc of 8″·7. Neither of these stars is however visible to the naked eye.

In Region 18 we also find the fine constellation Scorpio easily recognised by its brightest star Alpha Scorpii or Antares. The observer will note how Antares lies near one end of a chain of second and third magnitude stars. This constellation is just seen in the summer months from the latitudes of Great Britain and it contains some of the richest fields of the Milky Way. But it is in the Southern skies that the full splendour of Scorpio is developed. Antares is the ruddiest of all the conspicuous stars in the heavens, being next followed by Betelgeuze and then by Aldebaran.

Ara and Lupus are both inconsiderable groups of stars to the naked eye, though like every other part of the heavens they contain interesting telescopic objects. They will easily be identified from their position on Map II.

REGION 19.   SAGITTARIUS.

The two most conspicuous stars in Region 19 are both of the second magnitude. The first of these is Alpha Pavonis the lucida of the constellation Pavo. It may be easily recognised by the irregular quadrangle of which it forms one corner. The second conspicuous star is Alpha Gruis the lucida of the constellation Grus which constellation as a whole should be sought in the adjoining Region 14.

The most notable configuration in Region 19 is formed

by eight stars each about the third magnitude, and belonging to Sagittarius. The Milky Way is specially beautiful in this region. Near the star Gamma Sagittarius the stream becomes condensed into a vivid mass of stars so that in an area of about twenty-four square degrees the number of Milky Way stars exceeds 100,000, according to Sir John Herschel's computation.

In this part of its course the Milky Way contains innumerable objects well worth the attention of those possessed of good telescopes. There are places where the stars are so closely packed together as to form what must be described as clusters. Some of these are the very striking objects known as globular clusters. In this part of the heavenly river there are also Nebulae which no telescopic powers seem capable of resolving into stars.

As to the distances of the stars forming the Milky Way from the Earth we have little information, because the distances are too great to be certainly discoverable by our methods of measurement. But we may here record that the late Professor Newcomb estimated that these clustering masses of stars are so remote that the light they send us has needed 3000 years for its journey. Superb photographs of the Milky Way have been obtained by Professor E. E. Barnard at the Yerkes Observatory. Some of these display the structure of the Milky Way as it has never been seen by mere eye study even with the very finest telescopes. See p. 160.

Region 20. The South Pole.

Finally Region 20 includes those constellations which lie within 25° of the South Pole. It is therefore defined by a circle of which the South Pole is the centre. This important point is unfortunately not conspicuously shown as is the corresponding Pole in the Northern heavens. The North Pole is clearly indicated by the proximity of the bright and unmistakable Pole Star. No doubt near the South Pole there are multitudes of stars but not one of them is bright enough to serve as an obvious label for the South Pole.

Four celestial objects are specially noteworthy in Region 20. Two of them are second magnitude stars, and the third is the wonderful object in Dorado and Mensa called the great Nubecula, the fourth is the lesser Nubecula and the two objects are often spoken of as the Clouds of Magellan.

The two stars are known to astronomers as Alpha Trianguli Australis and Beta Argûs. They are nearly equidistant from the South Pole. The third conspicuous object is the great Nubecula and it will help to indicate the position of the South Pole. This unmarked point lies half way between Alpha Triang. Aust. and the centre of the great Nubecula. We may also note that an equilateral triangle has its vertices at the star Beta Argûs, the centre of the great Nubecula, and the South Pole.

The Nubeculae are conspicuously visible to the naked eye. Their degrees of brightness may be estimated by the statement that strong moonlight will totally obliterate the lesser Nubecula but not quite the greater.

When examined through telescopes of adequate power each of the Nubeculae shows a conglomeration of remarkable objects unparalleled in any other part of the heavens. In the greater Nubecula, there are 600 stars of the seventh, eighth, ninth, and tenth magnitudes and no fewer than 278 distinct clusters of smaller stars and nebulae have been enumerated.

There appears to be a fundamental difference in structure between the Clouds of Magellan and the luminous masses of the Milky Way notwithstanding the casual impression of their similarity given by a naked eye survey.

On the border of the Nubecula Minor lies a globular cluster of stars. It is visible to the naked eye with the lustre of a $4\frac{1}{2}$ magnitude star and when viewed through a powerful telescope has been described by Gould as "perhaps the most impressive object of the kind in either hemisphere." In the Nubecula Major there is a remarkable Nebula (30 Doradûs) faintly visible to the naked eye and shown to be a magnificent object of its class when viewed in the telescope. It is no doubt a notable spiral nebula.

INDEX.

(The numbers refer to the pages)

For EU product safety concerns, contact us at Calle de José Abascal, 56–1°, 28003 Madrid, Spain or eugpsr@cambridge.org.

 www.ingramcontent.com/pod-product-compliance
Ingram Content Group UK Ltd.
Pitfield, Milton Keynes, MK11 3LW, UK
UKHW012328130625
459647UK00009B/144